When it comes to integrity, it's easy to "talk the talk," but Millard Mac-Adam's new book recognizes how hard it is to "walk the walk." *Intentional Integrity* concentrates on "how to" specifics and the wonderful blessing that God has for those who follow His ethical standards.

It's a book worth reading.

—William L. Armstrong
Senator, Colorado

My favorite saying is, "You've got to be before you can do and do before you can have." *Intentional Integrity* teaches how to be—and the importance of being—the right kind of person in order to do the right kinds of things so you can have what's truly important. It's true that all great failures are character failures and here's a book on character that, if followed, will help eliminate the great failures and create great successes. Valuable information.

—Zig Ziglar
Chairman, The Zig Ziglar Corporation

Mac MacAdam is a committed business leader: committed to the Lord Jesus Christ and committed to helping Christians in business learn how to apply scriptural principles in the workplace. *Intentional Integrity* addresses a topic that is essential if we are to be "salt and light" in the world in which we live and work. In *Intentional Integrity*, you will find a treasury of practical and biblically based principles for making integrity central to your personal life and your business.

—Phil Downer
President, Christian Business Men's Committee of USA

This book confronts the issue of integrity head on. It is a tremendous practical guide addressing the critical issues of living a balanced, bountiful, and beneficial life. Millard MacAdam uses helpful tools for self-evaluation to help determine areas of our life that need attention. He shares relevant issues we all face and gives meaningful solutions to help us make responsible decisions in the area of integrity. I thoroughly enjoyed this book.

—Sylvia Nash
President, Christian Healthcare Network

Integrity seems to be the lost chord in our relativistic culture. Dr. Millard's new book *Intentional Integrity* is must reading for those who are committed to taking the high road. Successful people find out how the system works and then stay on the good side of how things work. *Intentional Integrity* lays out that path, hands you a road map, and invites you to join the journey.

—Joe C. Aldrich
President, Multnomah Bible College and Biblical Seminary

Integrity is a word for our times in every discipline—in politics, business, the professions—and particularly for the church. We who are Christians need to know that the foundation for integrity lies with God.

In this highly readable and enjoyable book, Mac MacAdam clearly and definitively demonstrates that integrity is an intentional grace to be sought by us if we are to live lives pleasing to God.

—Ted W. Engstrom
President Emeritus, World Vision

In a day when apparent guilt seems to be rewarded and the black and white of right and wrong have become gray at best—even in Christian circles—Millard MacAdam has produced a valuable tool in *Intentional Integrity*. By bringing us back to the scriptural foundations of our country and the absolutes of right and wrong, he lays out an important and workable plan for reintroducing integrity into every part of our lives—personal or professional, and therefore creating a balanced and beneficial life. The accountability of the PACT concept is a must for every Christian leader!

—Florence Littauer
President, CLASS Speakers, Inc.
Speaker/author

I am impressed with Millard MacAdam's vision and system. *Intentional Integrity* is not just a "can do" book, but a "you can change America" system that is applicable for every individual.

—Ray Miller
President, Fellowship of Companies for Christ, International

Millard MacAdam desires that we have a life worth living. That kind of life is not automatic. It comes through intentional strategies. In order to get and give the most in life, this thoughtful and practical book on bottom-line living is a must.

—John Tolson
President, The Gathering/USA, Inc.

Dr. Millard MacAdam issues a challenge for thoughtful, purposeful living that cannot be ignored. But he does not stop there. He answers the call with the principles and skills necessary for a balanced life. *Intentional Integrity* is a must read for today's leader—You!

—Beverly LaHaye
President, Concerned Women for America

INTENTIONAL
INTEGRITY

INTENTIONAL INTEGRITY

MILLARD MacADAM

ALIGNING YOUR LIFE WITH GOD'S VALUES

BROADMAN
&HOLMAN
PUBLISHERS

Nashville, Tennessee

4262-64
0-8054-6264-3

Published by Broadman & Holman Publishers
Nashville, Tennessee

Acquisitions and Development Editor: Vicki Crumpton
Interior Design by Leslie Joslin

Dewey Decimal Classification: 241
Subject Heading: CHRISTIAN LIFE / CHRISTIAN ETHICS
Library of Congress Card Catalog Number: 95-20861

Unless otherwise noted, Scripture quotations are from the Holy Bible, New International Version, copyright © 1973, 1978, 1984 by International Bible Society.

Library of Congress Cataloging-in-Publication Data
MacAdam, Millard N., 1930–
     Intentional integrity : aligning your life with God's values / Millard N. MacAdam
        p. cm.
     Includes bibliographical references.
     ISBN 0-8054-6264-3 (pb)
     1. Christian ethics. 2. Business—Religious aspects—Christianity. 3. Business ethics. 4. Success in business. 5. Success. 6. Christian life. I. Title.
BJ1275.M32   1996
241—dc20

95-20861
CIP

96 97 98 99 00 5 4 3 2 1

To all my fellow truth seekers along life's roadways.
Especially to all who have inspired, encouraged, and helped me during
my ongoing journey toward becoming a person of intentional integrity.
They have helped me value, develop, and maintain a
relatively balanced, bountiful, and beneficial life.

May God bless each of you richly as you let
Him guide you along your own journey.

CONTENTS

ACKNOWLEDGMENTS

Writing this book has helped me "let go and let God" use the Holy Spirit to guide and motivate me. During the times I felt inadequate to the task, "dry of thought," and emotionally and mentally burned out from writing, He filled me with renewed insight and determination.

I'm thankful for God's guidance, encouragement, and direction throughout the process of conceptualizing and writing this book. It would never have turned into a "labor of love," taken form, or been completed without God's help and guidance.

I want to thank my family members, friends, colleagues, and clients who encouraged me along this writing journey. Their encouraging remarks, thoughtful critiques, and creative ideas were invaluable.

I also want to express my gratitude for the help of others:

- Robert Tamasy, editor of *Contact* magazine for Christian Business Men's Committee USA, for coaching me as a writer over the years and for publishing the article that attracted Vicki Crumpton, my editor, to call me about doing a book.

- My wife, Barbara, for her reading, editing, comments, prayers, and prodding to keep on writing throughout the process.

- My son-in-law, Dayne Burns, for his editorial comments and encouragement over the years. Dayne has been after me to write books on several different topics and has helped me maintain the staying power to complete this one.

- All of the people who shared stories from their lives with me for inclusion in the book. They added a personal touch, deeper meaning, and reader motivation. I believe their stories will give encouragement to my readers.

- The many business, education, and religious authors and speakers whose messages, research, and writings have challenged, edified, and enriched my own thinking. They have contributed to my growth as a consultant and facilitator as well as strengthened my commitment to be a person of integrity. There is not enough space to mention them all. However, I do want to recognize those whose prolific speaking and writing has helped me the most over the professional and personal ministry years of my life: Warren Benis, William Bennett, Kenneth Blanchard, Peter Block, Charles Colson, Stephen Covey, Gene Getz, Tom Gordon, Ted Engstrom, Florence Littauer, John MacArthur, Burt Nanus, Bob Shank, and Charles Swindoll.

May God richly bless each one of you!

INTRODUCTION

You're driving down the interstate at 65 mph. You notice a vibration in your steering wheel, and your car veers slightly to the left or right as you round the next bend. You apply your brakes and the vibration rattles your teeth. What's wrong? The wheels are out of alignment, causing a smooth road to turn into a washboard and your straight course to weave from side to side.

The same is true when you're riding down life's trails—your life can get out of alignment. If you're like me when this happens, you'll find it feels more like trying to ride a unicycle than driving a car! Unicycles are unforgiving, the skills required to navigate them more demanding, the mental, physical, and emotional strength more critical to ride over steep grades and bumpy terrain. You can topple over at any moment if you fail to pay attention to the road, to every detail of your personal balance, or fail to carefully maintain the alignment of the hub, spokes, and wheel.

Just like your car or imaginary unicycle, life can manifest symptoms when things get out of balance: Days that should have gone smoothly don't. Little incidents at work—what someone says, assignments uncompleted, calls not returned—begin to get under your skin. Then you go home. The bumps and ruts grow into bickering, fighting, and wounded feelings—sure signs of a life out of balance.

The key to building a balanced life—one that is aligned with your godly values—is the practice of *intentional integrity*. In this book you'll explore strategies for helping you intentionally build greater integrity into all aspects of your life and the lives of those around you. You'll see how you can have a better family life and career success by committing to being a person of intentional integrity who consistently applies proven, traditional ethical standards to his or her conduct. You'll see how focusing on people before profits, power, prestige, and pleasure will serve you, your family, and your employer. You'll be fortified with key strategies from my Total Integrity Management^SM System. These will help you align your Wheel of Life and avoid the pitfalls of the operational paradigm of conditional integrity. You'll be better able to stand strong and not compromise your personal character, competence, and commitment to do what's right when under fire.

I've heard a lot of talks and read a lot of books on the subjects of ethics, integrity, and balancing one's life. Everything I heard and read always omitted two critical components: firm ethical *standards for conduct* and a genuine, *personal accountability process* involving groups of people.

In sharing with you what I've learned, I'll be drawing heavily on my experiences as a husband to my wife, Barbara, since 1951, as a father helping to raise three children to adulthood, and as a grandfather trying to encourage and help guide six wonderful grandchildren—two finishing their second year of college! I'll also draw on the experiences I've had as a business person and educator. These include being a teacher, school principal, and personnel director, as well as the CEO of a small start-up service company shortly after I turned twenty-five.

I've learned the value of possessing proactive character traits the hard way. These tough learning experiences have motivated me to develop more patience to replace my reactive behavior and to work more diligently at keeping my life in balance by using godly values.

Proactive and *reactive* are common terms in leadership circles today. *Proactive* means we effectively initiate things—we plan how to take appropriate and worthwhile action before being told or expected to do so. *Reactive* means that we aren't prepared to respond appropriately to circumstances and flail away at people and react to events.

When I've acted in *reactive* ways as a husband, father, manager, or consultant, I've been a destructive person! When I've thought, talked, and acted in *proactive* ways, made the right decisions, and responded in the right ways, I've found that I've served as a *developer*—developer of character, competence, and commitment in myself and others.

As you begin implementing the processes, tools, and strategies in this book, you'll experience the personal benefits and satisfaction that comes from a commitment to intentional integrity in all dimensions of your life. You'll also position yourself to enjoy the spiritual as well as the economic benefits that can be gained from living a more integrated, ethical, balanced, and beneficial life.

PERSONAL INTEGRITY MANAGEMENT

In this book you'll discover how you can free yourself from the destructive trap set by what I call "the big lie virus of dishonesty." Too many people have capitulated to *conditional integrity* . . . being honest when it's convenient and as long as it doesn't cost personally. This operational paradigm is often touted as "the way to succeed" in life, marriage, and business; yet every day we see the tragic results of selective dishonesty. While this paradigm may seem innocent enough at first glance, the "smaller" lies, deceptions, and improprieties people commit build callousness and too often lead to the fraud and outright theft that destroys individual careers, families, businesses, and other institutions.

People who elect to live their lives within this paradigm lack the core operating values they need to guide their conduct. They avoid any kind of workable mutual accountability process to stay on track and help themselves and those close to them build balanced lives.

In contrast to conditional integrity, intentional integrity will give every area of your life a solid foundation for honest and truthful actions. Intentional integrity insists that there are absolutes, there is a right and a wrong, and that we can know the difference. Intentional integrity means that we hold ourselves accountable and encourage others to hold us accountable for our actions. We do what is right, not what is convenient or painless.

BUILDING A BALANCED LIFE

I will use a wheel metaphor throughout this book. Picture yourself on a unicycle, negotiating the ups and downs of the road. The wheel on your unicycle is your "Wheel of Life" with ten different spokes or dimensions that provide the structure for the wheel. The selected strategies and tools from my Total Integrity Management^{SM} System will offer ways to help you keep your balance, move forward, and keep you going smoothly at the speed you want to go.

THE PATH TO INTENTIONAL INTEGRITY AND A BALANCED LIFE

As you examine strategies for aligning your life, you'll discover how you can steer a straighter course. You'll learn how you can "safety-equip" yourself with tough-minded, warmhearted Personal Accountability and Commitment Team partners at home, church, and work. You'll discover how you can personally develop and reinforce high integrity practices and the traditional ethical standards for conduct and character that God has outlined (and you've elected to follow) as your standards for living.

You'll also have the opportunity to examine how much you value the traditional ethical standards for conduct God has set out for us. You'll explore some easy-to-use Total Integrity Management tools and strategies that will strengthen your abilities as a service-oriented, value-driven leader at home and work.

Chapter 1 will clarify the problem of dishonesty leading to conditional integrity. Chapter 2 will offer the solution, intentional integrity supported by Personal Integrity Management tools and strategies. In chapter 3 you'll take stock of your life. Assessing the balance of ten areas—or spokes on your wheel. You'll find out which areas are balanced and which areas need alignment. In chapter 4 you'll develop your "main bearings" for the "hub" of your Wheel of Life . . . your purpose statement (a written statement of the purpose God has for you and all of His children), and a life vision statement (a word-picture of what your life can and should look like as you use your unique, God-given gifts and talents to achieve God's purpose for your life).

You'll also develop the remaining bearings for your hub, life operating values and a credo statement (a list describing the key, Spirit-driven operating values that you'll honor and live by as you work to achieve your life purpose and vision). Chapter 5 begins the process of defining your mission statements for each segment of your life (a written statement about what you are going to do to, and/or with, whom, and how); your goals (the broadly stated written targets that you establish to enhance and/or align each dimension of your life so you achieve your mission); and performance objectives (the written, measurable action steps you'll take or tasks you'll do that will incrementally contribute to the achievement of a specific goal) for two spokes.

As you move into chapter 6 and the remaining chapters, the focus shifts to personal integrity management skills you can use to strengthen your life. The balancing process continues as each chapter also gives you an opportunity to develop your mission statements, your goals, and your performance objectives for the remaining spokes.

One intent of this book is to guide and encourage you as you develop the mission and goals for each dimension of your life. Another is to help you align them so they work in concert with each of the others.

The tools and strategies will help you keep your Wheel of Life in good alignment. These tools and strategies will focus on helping you to strengthen each particular dimension of your life as you keep each spoke aligned with your hub—your purpose, vision, and values.

GETTING READY

Before you start, I encourage you to organize a notebook for writing down your thoughts and feelings and keeping track of your commitments to specific action steps. Your notebook will become a valuable tool to review for information, to reflect on previous decisions, and to affirm the progress you make toward developing a more balanced, bountiful, and beneficial life.

Divide your notebook into sections for each chapter. Simple chapter tab titles might be (1) Conditional Integrity, (2) Intentional Integrity, (3) Taking Stock, (4) The Hub, (5) Mission & Goals, (6) Follower Skills, (7) Leadership Skills, (8) Adaptive Skills, (9) Peacemaker Skills, (10) Communication Skills, (11) Mutual Accountability Skills, (12) Change Facilitation Skills, and (13) Maintaining Your Truing Process.

Next, create sections for each dimension of your life. Simple tab titles might be (1) Spiritual (2) Intellectual, (3) Career, (4) Community, (5) Recreational, (6) Financial, (7) Fitness, (8) Social, (9) Family, and (10) Emotional.

In these sections you can keep your mission statement, goals, and objectives for each dimension of your life as well as special surveys, notes, concerns and possibilities, resource articles, or anything useful to you in developing and maintaining that particular dimension.

TIME OUT! *Put your notebook together*

Throughout the chapters I'll give you some TIME OUTS! for you to reflect and write in the log portion of your notebook. In other TIME OUT! periods you will be asked to take time to complete specific activities.

Part 1

BECOMING A PERSON OF INTENTIONAL INTEGRITY

1

CONDITIONAL INTEGRITY: A CORRUPTING CRISIS

Over two thousand years ago God gave King Solomon wisdom and much more because Solomon asked God for wisdom instead of riches and power. Solomon valued wisdom, as he told us in Proverbs 3:13–18: "Blessed is the man who finds wisdom, the man who gains understanding, for she is more profitable than silver and yields better returns than gold. She is more precious than rubies; nothing you desire can compare with her. Long life is in her right hand; in her left hand are riches and honor. Her ways are pleasant ways, and all her paths are peace. She is a tree of life to those who embrace her; those who lay hold of her will be blessed."

Wise people know right from wrong, *act wisely on what they know,* and demonstrate good judgment. In the long run, they will be happier than people who are merely rich with material things. The value of wisdom comes home to me when I read about the lives of rich people like Ivan Boesky, Howard Hughes, Charles Keating, and Donald Trump. Have you found anything that compares to wisdom? For me nothing has compared with it; and where I have acted wisely it has rewarded me with the long, good life; riches, honor, pleasure, and peace Solomon talked about.

Think about this statement adapted from a quotation attributed to Peter Drucker: "People might know too little, perform poorly, lack judgment and ability, and yet not do too much damage. But if they lack in character and integrity . . . no matter how knowledgeable, how brilliant, how successful, . . . they destroy. They destroy people, the most valuable resource of the enterprise. They destroy spirit. And they destroy performance."

We are becoming increasingly tolerant of lack of integrity in the organizations for which we work and in the organizations that serve us. We are no longer shocked at the flagrant, open, and often hostile disrespect for the traditional values that made America great. With ever-growing cynicism, we have come to expect dishonesty!

Daily we can read about the breakdown of integrity in educational, religious, governmental, and business organizations. Most of us can tell our own stories. Does it hit closer to home when a colleague is caught embezzling? When a competitor gets the contract because he or she bribed or lied? When an associate commits adultery and demolishes his or her marriage and family?

Several years ago I began to study the impact that ethical standards, or the lack thereof, have had on careers and companies. I interviewed people involved in different unethical situations in large and small organizations. For the most part, these people could not identify a firm standard for right and wrong action. They did not comprehend the notion of moral absolutes and thought that whatever they chose to do was right.

Who sets the standard? We all encounter different levels of "truth" and "righteousness" in our lives. First, there is self-made truth, the truth I experience in my mind and heart from values, education, and events I've encountered. Second, there is culture-made truth, laws of the land, theories of science, norms of our institutions, and our society as a whole. Third, there are natural laws, or God-made truth, of which all humanity is aware and too often disobeys. For instance, the natural or God-made law of gravity is obvious to us and more likely to be obeyed by all. The God-made laws for relationships are clearly stated in the Bible, however they are disobeyed by Christian and non-Christian alike.

What happens when you and I intentionally distance ourselves from the reality inherent in natural or God-made truths or laws? What happens when we base our thoughts, words, and actions on the illusionary self-made or culture-made truths? We end up in a pit of dysfunction and destruction!

Take for instance the current debate over violence in video games. People who oppose censorship say we cannot determine a standard of violence or pornography in the videos, therefore we must not regulate them. By that logic, it would be okay for you and me to discriminate against minorities or engage in criminal acts because we cannot set a reality-based standard of right and wrong. What's the result of this "can't set a standard" mentality? We see that media organizations, television companies, and recording companies take license and glorify, promote, and reinforce mankind's lowest, degrading forms of lust, greed, violence, and deviant behavior. They promote them as normal and the "in" thing to do!

CONDITIONAL INTEGRITY: THE CORRUPTING OF LEADERS

Far too many of the individuals who occupy positions of leadership in America's families, schools, churches, businesses, and local, state, and national governments appear to be mesmerized by, and practice, the modern-day operational paradigm of *conditional integrity*, perhaps because this paradigm makes it easier for them to justify lowering their ethical standards for conduct and helps soothe their weak consciences.

This conditional way of thinking about integrity comes from a school of thought that emerged in the sixties. It promotes the idea that anything is okay as long as it doesn't hurt someone else. This tragic way of thinking, however, is illogical and inconsistent. It has contributed to the dishonest, destructive behaviors that bring about cultural and financial decay. In a nutshell, people who think about integrity from a conditional perspective more often than not behave dishonestly.

The "official" leaders in the homes, institutions, and businesses of America who have bought in to this conditional way of thinking about integrity receive low grades on trust from those whom they serve and employ. Their actions have contributed to the disintegration of others' lives as well as the organizations that employ them. They have failed to lead effectively because they have failed to be honest, to model high integrity, and to live balanced lives.

Conditional integrity is a destructive paradigm and is driven and spread by the virus of dishonesty. Conditional integrity creates delusions that ultimately lead people into "moral quicksand." Sadly, this slipshod, wimpy stance on integrity and ethical standards for conduct is being consciously and unconsciously reinforced, and even promoted, in many of America's schools, media, business, educational, and even religious institutions and families. We, and generations to come, will continue to reap the negative consequences of conditional integrity. However, by raising up a critical mass of integrity champions, we can change this direction.

Conditional integrity has contributed greatly to bringing about the following consequences in many of our governmental organizations, churches, schools, and businesses.

- Inconsistent behavior, performance, and productivity
- Distrust
- Disloyalty
- Low levels of motivation
- Low productivity potential
- Poor profits and/or cash losses
- Lying and theft
- Drug abuse
- Adultery and divorce
- Murder and suicide

Daily we read stories about people who demonstrate these behaviors. The deeds we read about are too serious and too frequent for us to assume they are isolated reports about a small number of dishonest people.

Consider a sampling of trends and events:

IN EDUCATION

Over recent decades our colleges and universities have been heavily influenced by business. They have become increasingly market-driven, accepting grants and endowments for curricula mainly centered on the sciences and business and eliminating curricula exploring the ethical and moral foundations of our society. This has motivated educators to move away from the development of character and broad-based competencies toward producing a narrow range of competencies in business and science.

As we face major problems with the unemployable masses and the undependable in the work force, we should look back a decade at the report, *A Nation at Risk*. It reported that 23 million adults and about 13 percent of all seventeen-year-olds were functionally illiterate. That was a decade ago!

Teaching standards for ethical and moral conduct and the work ethic our country was founded on continue to fade from America's classrooms. Isn't it time to ask, "Who are the champions of character and competence development?" when we read about

- a state superintendent of schools ousted for illegal use of funds;
- a school district business manager who embezzled $4 million and went to jail;
- a teacher ousted and lost his credentials for molesting children;
- a university professor who falsified research records to keep grant money flowing;
- a school district superintendent falsified attendance records to get tax money.

IN RELIGION

Almost a decade ago George Gallup reported that church attendance makes little difference in people's ethical views and behavior. He determined that religious people lie, cheat, and pilfer as much as the nonreligious.[1] Are we better or worse today when we read that

- a television evangelist is imprisoned for sexual misconduct and fraud;
- a religious leader is convicted for child molestation;
- a church elder is convicted of fraud, theft, and perjury;

- a professed Christian executive of an auto firm is indicted for receiving bribes;
- a ministry organization leader paid himself an extravagant salary and expenses.

IN GOVERNMENT

Almost a decade ago, the U.S. Justice Department reported a comparison of indictments and convictions of federal officials between 1975 and 1985. This report showed that the "sleaze factor" was more prevalent in our capital than ever before. In 1975 the department recorded 53 indictments and 43 convictions. In 1985, only one decade later, the department reported 563 indictments and 470 convictions of federal officials. As you review recent reports in your newspaper, you may ask, "Is it better or worse today?" when you read that

- a local water district manager was ousted because of "favors and gifts" received;
- a senator used influence to protect wrongdoing in the savings and loan industry;
- a president covered up illegal acts of government and military colleagues;
- a police chief is ousted as charges of rape and sexual harassment are filed;
- a Department of Defense officer is convicted of receiving bribes from defense company executives.

IN BUSINESS

A decade ago, crime on Wall Street was at an all-time high. National best-seller *Den of Thieves* by Pulitzer Prize winner James B. Stewart reported the actions of Ivan Boesky, Martin Siegel, Michael Milken, and Dennis Levine. These characters head a cast of other insider trading scandal participants who epitomize the abuse of the term *freedom*. Boesky knew he was committing a crime and even anticipated the $100-million dollar penalty in order to make money from the deal.[2] And the examples multiply:

- a medical center director was put in prison and fined for bribery and fraud;

- a top CPA firm paid $312 million to settle negligence charges over bank audits;
- a national retail firm's auto repair department was cited for cheating customers;
- a tobacco firm falsified research reports and secretly added addictive chemicals;
- a major oil company was exposed for covering up oil spills over a forty-year period.

IN SPORTS

Historically, sports and sportsmanship were supposed to go hand-in-hand. Participating in sports was a way to develop character and discipline in students. Professionals played their sport in "Olympic style" with a spirit of doing their best on the playing field with fairness and good conduct.

Now our television screens and sports arenas publicly honor teams, managers, and players who climb financial peaks while falling into moral valleys. The examples multiply day by day:

- a top athlete is convicted of drugs and rape;
- a college sports manager is fined for "buying" players;
- a Little League coach lies about his players' ages to give him a winning advantage;
- fans throw bottles at the opposing players on the field;
- a basketball star gets AIDS from promiscuous, unprotected sex, encouraging "safe sex" over fidelity.

IN ENTERTAINMENT

There was a day when clean entertainment was the norm. Most movies, plays, and stage shows were places you could take your kids. Now some stage plays are often explicit, plain filthy, and disgusting. Sexist jokes and innuendo are found on many daytime radio talk and music shows. Our record industry produces more dirty stuff than ever before. We can even get 900 "dial-a-sex" on our phones.

Pornography abounds in the name of legitimate entertainment. Attempts to stop the flood bring out the legal hawks to defend the production of videos, films, and magazines involving adults and young children. Where are we going?

- a topless bar opened in a "good" part of town with little resistance from citizens;
- violent movies showed explicit rape, killing, and sex play at the local theater;
- a stage play portraying abnormal sex hide behind the claim of "art";
- television produced prime-time shows that glorify sex out of wedlock and infidelity;
- an art gallery displayed a desecration of the American flag in the name of art.

IN FAMILIES

The home has historically and rightfully been the center for modeling, teaching, and instilling worthwhile values and morals in children. Increasingly, parents have ignored, delegated, or abdicated this important function to schools. It is here that too many educators are either ignorant of what is right and wrong from God's perspective or are afraid to teach the traditional ethical standards for conduct. When you look over the tragic family stories in your newspaper you may ask, "Is it better or worse today?" as you see that

- a father was sued by his daughters for seven years of incest and rape;
- a battered wife killed her husband in a state of fear and anger;
- a starving child was locked in a closet by his parents for discipline purposes;
- a baby was beaten to death and his mother sent to prison;
- a father and mother were convicted for heading a drug-selling operation.

WHEN DID TRADITIONAL JUDEO-CHRISTIAN VALUES BEGIN TO DECLINE?

Numerous writers and speakers give historical perspectives on the virus of dishonesty and how it has penetrated the thinking and actions of a majority of our country's Supreme Court members over the last several decades. I'd like to summarize what appear to have been critical incidences of wrong thinking and actions on the part of some individuals who have filled the seats of our Supreme Court in years past and some benchmarks of decline that appear to correlate with their wrong thinking and actions: They are from a July 4th address by Charles Stanley.[3]

Please consider this umbrella: "What a blessed nation we live in." You and I enjoy God-given soil, climate, and resources that contribute to a unique free-enterprise system that provides opportunities to the poor to become rich. It has allowed creative, industrious, and high-integrity people to make worthwhile contributions and live quality lives.

America was already a blessed land when it was inhabited by the Indians and then discovered by Columbus. In addition to the blessings of incredible natural resources, it was later blessed with the seeds of freedom planted by our founding fathers. Most of these godly men, their wives, and their families stood for truth and taught the gospel. They believed what the Bible said, "Blessed is the nation whose God is the Lord."

They founded our country with the intent that our government and laws would always be based on biblical principles. In 1811, two decades after the First Amendment was established, this statement was made by the majority of the Supreme Court: "Whatever strikes at the root of Christianity tends to destroy civil government."

As the foundations for the government of our country were being laid, James Madison said, "We have staked the whole future of American civilization, not on the power of government, far from it. The future of America is not in this new document, it's not in the Constitution. We have staked the future of all of our political institutions upon the capacity of each and every one of us to govern ourselves according to the Ten Commandments."

Lincoln kept this biblical foundation for government in view when he said, "It is the duty of nations as well as men to recognize the truth, announced in Holy Scripture and proven by all of history that those nations only are blessed whose God is the Lord."

Near the turn of the century in 1892 the Supreme Court reinforced the source of the principles for law and government our founding fathers put in place. The court stated, "Our laws and our institutions must necessarily be based on and must include the teachings of the redeemer of mankind, which could be none other than the person of Jesus Christ."

Today 95 percent of America's citizens say they believe in God, and our money is still imprinted with "In God We Trust." However, if you examine the textbooks used in our schools and universities you'll find they have been stripped of the words of our founding leaders when they referred to things related to God's Word.

A group of scholars examined 15,000 original documents to identify quotations from important people identified with the founding of our country. They found 34 percent of the quotations came from the Bible, 60 percent from conclusions based on the Word of God. Ninety-four percent of the quotations identified from men of this period were based on the Bible.

Was this a major turning point ? At the time of World War II, the integrity of the collective thinking and actions of the majority of men on the Supreme Court appears to have changed radically as new appointments were made. In 1947 the majority of men on the Court, appearing to ignore our historical past and with *no stated precedent*, declared that it was not the government's responsibility to protect the church and that the church should stay out of government. They paid no attention to the fact that there was no mention of separation of church and state in the First Amendment!

As rebellion began to explode in the sixties, the men on the Court appear to have engaged in illogical, wrong thinking, and piece by piece, tore out the foundation stones that provided the guidelines for recognizing good character among people and the intents for the laws of America. They began dismantling the sources for the governmental and legal foundation our founding fathers had so carefully put in place with an eye and heart on God's Holy Word.

In 1962 the majority of men sitting on the Court declared no prayer in the schools, again with no precedent or legal reason. In 1963 the majority of men sitting on the Court ordered the removal of the Bible from schools, again without precedent or law or reading or questioning the basis on which this nation was founded. This was their statement, "If portions of the New Testament were read without explanation, they could be, and have been, psychologically harmful to a child."

In 1977 the majority of men sitting on the Court recognized atheism as a religion. In 1980 the majority of men sitting on the Court ordered that the Ten Commandments be removed from the walls of classrooms throughout America. The Court's statement was: "If the Ten Commandments were to have any effect at all, it would be to induce students to read them. And if they read them they will meditate on them and if they meditate on them they will respect them and obey them and that would be unconstitutional." In 1986 the majority of men sitting on the Court recognized secular humanism as a religion.

Step by step the majority of men sitting on the Supreme Court, without precedent or law on its side, gave an open forum to evil, godless religions. It tried to make Christianity and the biblical principles that guided the foundation of our country impotent.

One might ask, "Where was I when all of this was happening? Where were all the legal minds? (My dad was a lawyer and I never heard him question the situation!) What was in the minds of men and women in Congress? Shouldn't they have been challenging the members of the Supreme Court for exchanging one religion at the exclusion of another . . . secular humanism for Christianity?"

It may be by accident, but during the decades after prayer, the Bible, and the Ten Commandments were removed from schools by the highest court in our land, we have seen increasing levels of divorce, violence and crime, illegal use of drugs, teenage pregnancies, abortions, and illiteracy.

As we place ourselves above God and try to become self-sufficient, free of all moral restraint, we seem to be moving deeper into the depths of moral and spiritual confusion and social breakdown.

IT IS TIME TO STOP THINKING, SAYING, AND DOING THE WRONG THING!

The virus of dishonesty is spreading like an out-of-control cancer into the minds and hearts of children and adults. Why has the integrity crisis worsened? I believe it is because masses of America's adults and youth, Christians and non-Christians, are out of touch with what is right and wrong from God's perspective—from His reality, based on His truth. They are either ignorant of or reject the proven biblical standards for conduct on which America's Constitution, laws, and free enterprise system were founded.

Where do we find these traditional, ethical standards for conduct? Throughout the Bible! Review the Ten Commandments and examine how they have served as the foundation blocks for living, for our country's constitution and original laws, and for the codes of conduct found in many of America's outstanding companies. Read through the Sermon on the Mount, carefully examine the Beatitudes and the Golden Rule and you'll be hard-pressed to be confused about what's right and what's wrong conduct. Ponder 1 Corinthians 13 and Galatians 5:22–26 and you'll be clear on what the manifestations of a loving character are and are not. Read through the Books of Proverbs and Ephesians.

Great numbers of us, in all walks of life, do not live our lives in line with these traditional standards for ethical conduct. Too many of us have embraced the modern-day, conditional approach to integrity. As a result, we too often capitulate to the virus of dishonesty and lower our standards for conduct. We, too often, take wrong action when the pressure is on in order to gain a false sense of personal advantage.

If you or I choose to operate within the modern-day operational paradigm of conditional integrity, we'll be nurturing ethical compromise. We will be causing the virus of dishonesty to flourish because we have not made the decision to do the right thing ahead of time. Moral immaturity is motivated by personal profit, prestige, or pleasure instead of intentionally deciding to do what's right. Compromising our character occurs when we underestimate evil and flirt with, and capitulate to, temptations of all kinds. Compromising our character is always just a choice away; it is enticed through flattery and fantasy. It ensnares us and brings about dishonest rationalizations and deceptions when we refuse to think about the rightness of our actions.

It is time for us to *intentionally* focus on God's proven values and principles for living and working and commit to the Total Integrity Management of all segments of our lives. Then we will gain the maximum benefits of a balanced life and make this world a better place to live.

TIME OUT! *Reflect on:*
What? So What? and Now What?

Key Reflections

1. What do you see and experience as the factors in the integrity crisis?
2. What is it doing to you and how are you part of it?
3. What will you do to be part of the solution by obeying God's principles for living?

2

INTENTIONAL INTEGRITY: GOD'S PARADIGM FOR LIVING

Lou Hager is a property manager. Lou held a $40,000 a year position as superintendent of maintenance. He reported to the vice-president of property management. Lou's boss was a back-slapping, foul-mouthed individual who consistently pushed Lou to negotiate his people's salaries downward. He would page Lou at midnight after a fourteen-hour day, showing no concern for Lou's rest or family life. Lou's integrity came under fire when his boss ordered him to buy materials like carpet and paint and deliver it to his personal residence . . . while entering the tab on the bill sent to the owner of the properties being managed.

Because Lou was intentional about his integrity, he couldn't do it and told his boss so. Lou quit. The president of the company called him to find out what had happened. Lou told him; but a second wrong was committed—the president wasn't willing to do anything for fear of losing a vice-president that "made things happen."

Lou kept his integrity intact and got a new position in a company with sound ethical standards for doing business. He was happy and relieved to be out of the former environment. Later he found out that he and other employees would receive several hundred dollars in back pay as a result of a labor board investigation initiated by another employee of the company. He also watched as the unethical practices of the vice-president and the lack of courage of the president brought the company into bankruptcy. Over the long haul, what goes around comes around.

A COMMITMENT TO INTEGRITY

Let's start where the rubber meets the road: your commitment to being a person of intentional integrity. By maintaining your commitment and this focus, you'll begin the process of immunizing yourself with God's truths against the virus of dishonesty.

If intentional integrity seems like a difficult commitment, it is! God has warned us about trying to worship two masters. Yet God calls us to a high standard of conduct. Jesus told us in Matthew 5:48, "Be perfect, therefore, as your heavenly father is perfect." Peter also told us in 1 Peter 1:15–16 "But just as he who called you is holy, so be holy in all you do; for it is written: Be holy, because I am holy." Emphasizing the need for consistency between faith and conduct, James admonished us in James 1:22, "Do not merely listen to the word, and so deceive yourselves. Do what it says."

Warren W. Wiersbe stated it well in his book, *The Integrity Crisis*, when he said, "Jesus made it clear that integrity involves the whole of the inner person: the heart, the mind, and the will. The person with integrity has a single heart. He doesn't try to love God and the world at the same time. . . . The person with integrity also has a single mind, and single outlook ("eye") that keeps life going in the right direction . . . . Jesus also said that the person with integrity has a single will; he seeks to serve but one master."[4]

THE PRACTICALITY OF INTENTIONAL INTEGRITY

Integrity is the principle that gives bridges, buildings, companies, families, and people their wholeness, quality and strength. The word comes from the Latin *integras* which means "sound, whole, complete."

None of us would drive across a bridge if we knew the steel in the structure lacked integrity or the bolts were not tightened or the cement was not mixed properly. The same applies to a house we are ready to buy or office space in a high-rise building we are about to rent. We now have over 35 million laws to try to protect us from those of low integrity. Without integrity people and bridges suffer from a lack of soundness, wholeness, and completeness and are vulnerable to collapse or failure.

Do you ever think about issues of integrity where you work? Did you think about it before you got hired? Did you think about the consequences a lack of integrity within the organization's leadership, managerial, marketing, sales, employee service, and customer service functions could have on you and your career?

How important is the issue of integrity to the well-being of your family? What about family relationships, interpersonal communication, your budgeting process, your family problem-solving process or healthy food purchases?

What about the integrity of a person? Do you want to depend on services or products produced by people of low integrity? Do you want to be associated with them? Do you want to trust your life to them?

While we can't control the integrity of others, we can influence and inspire them by making sure our own integrity is as intact as possible. Modeling perfect integrity is one way Jesus so effectively taught others and why He wants us to follow Him and be salt and light in all dimensions of our lives.

FACE-TO-FACE WITH INTEGRITY

A few years ago I hired a secretary who was transferred from another department in a large public agency to help my consulting and training team with a major project. There was no doubt she had the skills to do excellent work for the project. She was outwardly friendly, and I thought she would fit in well with the group. Her former supervisor was pleased with her, but the type of work she had been doing in his department was no longer needed.

After a month on the job it was clear to me and our team that she was an albatross. It appeared her goal was to diligently work at avoiding work. I felt betrayed and was on a slow, controlled burn. I knew she had the "can do" to do the work, because I had checked it out with performance tests.

I started regularly reviewing the expectations I had laid out before hiring her. I tightly supervised and coached her, using all of the management and supervision tools at my command to try to help her become productive. I became angrier and angrier about the situation.

I blamed her for our project falling behind and felt she had been dishonest with me during the interview and assessment process. Finally, I verbally blasted her in front of the entire team at one of our staff meetings. It was embarrassing.

Things got worse. She continued to manipulate the environment to her advantage and did less and less work. I finally developed my documentation for her dismissal. I lost because of her previous glowing evaluations from others and she was transferred to another department.

When my rationalizing and anger had subsided, I reviewed this hiring mistake. Where had I gone wrong? How had I continued to go wrong? How could I avoid this in the future?

I came to realize that I had diligently evaluated regarding her "can do" competencies. What I had failed to check out was her "will do" motivation to work in a fast-paced, high energy, high demand training environment. When she didn't work out in the job, the virus of dishonesty attacked me. Rather than look inward and accept the responsibility of where I had failed to do due diligence in hiring her, I became angry and blamed her.

As I backtracked through her previous work situations, I discovered that she had been functioning in bureaucratic environments where little was expected in the way of work production. She had never faced tight time demands or sudden changes in materials. Others verified that she had high motivation for social involvement and friendships. The settings she had been in gave her ample opportunity to socialize, talk, and make phone calls to friends. She probably assumed that working on our project, since it was in the same public agency, would be the same. It wasn't, so she didn't and couldn't produce work at the level we needed.

Since this episode, I have diligently used surveys and computer technology to determine the "will do" factors of a potential employee. In addition to the competency requirements, I've made clear the operating values and norms to potential new hires and invited them to visit, talk to others, and assess for themselves if the environment supports their personal motivational needs.

TIME OUT! *Reflect on:*
What? So What? and Now What?

Key Reflections

1. What will it take for you to choose to be a Total Integrity Management champion?
2. What are the benefits of having intent and commitment to being a person of integrity?
3. What action steps will you take to "notch up" your integrity?

YOU'RE NEEDED AS AN INTEGRITY CHAMPION

The integrity crisis can be turned around by ordinary people like you and me who are committed to having open hearts, willing spirits, and an intent to think, say, and do the right things to strengthen the integrity of every aspect of our lives.

As an integrity champion, you will serve as a model at home and in the marketplace. You will demonstrate the stability and contribution that's possible when a person thinks, says, and does what is right. I'm pleased that you're committing yourself to being an important member of this group of integrity champions.

Fortunately, there are many others on the integrity journey. My favorite story about practical and value-driven business leaders came out of the Johnson and Johnson Tylenol tragedies. The account of these integrity champions is told well, and in detail, in Tom Haggai's book, *How the Best Was Won*.[5]

The tragedy of poisoned Tylenol hit Johnson and Johnson twice, in 1982 and again in 1986. Given their respected position and company credo that said, "Never offer for sale any product that might prove to be a hazard to a person's health," high-integrity decisions were made based on the values deeply inculcated into the company culture. Company chairman Jim Burke wanted to uncover convincing evidence to support his contention that focusing on integrity and expecting high ethical standards for conduct and morality when making corporate decisions was good business financially.

Burke's staff worked with The Business Round Table's Task Force on Corporate Responsibility and the Ethics Resource Center in Washington, D.C., to compile a list of twenty-six companies that met the criteria for ethical, high-integrity companies. The compounded growth of these companies was 10.7 percent over a thirty-year period, which was 1.34 times the growth of our GNP; and GNP was 10 times greater than it was thirty years before. The net income of these companies turned out to be 21.2 percent greater than average. If you and I had made an investment of $30,000 thirty years before in the composite of the Dow Jones, we would have received $134,000 on our investment. If we had invested in those companies that the study identified, our investment of $30,000 would have given us a return of $1,310,714.[6]

High-integrity companies driven by high ethical standards for conduct are far more successful financially over the long term. I believe the same holds true for individuals, their families, and their careers.

BENEFITS OF MANAGING YOUR LIFE, FAMILY, AND BUSINESS WITH INTEGRITY

Smaller companies that are the "integrity" brothers and sisters of the twenty-six companies reported above also have excellent profit records over the long term. They, too, experience longevity and develop value-added assets by the time they are sold. These smaller companies are also led by ethical, high-integrity leaders who expect highly ethical practices from all who participate in their enterprises. They model what they expect.

A shining example is Wetherill and Associates, Inc. (WAI), an automobile starter replacement parts company in Pennsylvania. The company's founding president and top management team have strictly adhered to the Right Action Ethic™ they incorporated into the company culture from the beginning. "Think, say, and do the right thing" is their simple but powerful personal and business credo. By diligently following their credo over a fourteen-year period, they've enjoyed growing to $120 million plus in annual revenues. They were selected as the number-one customer focus company by MCI and *Inc.* magazine in 1994. Their company has experienced low employee turnover and high customer loyalty. Everyone—managers, employees, suppliers, and customers—is encouraged to challenge any personal or corporate practices which are not perceived as doing the right thing; and the company's team of managers and employees make every effort to make things right for everyone.

The privilege of working with quality leaders in all types and sizes of organizations, like WAI, has allowed me to gain insight and proven strategies for developing the components of the Total Integrity Management™ System. I've observed these leaders as they carried out key functions in their companies with a focus on intentional integrity.

Leaders who practice intentional integrity have demonstrated to me over and over again that "good folks" don't finish last! I've seen how they set standards and expect the same from others.

They truly discern the difference between freedom and license. They expect to be held accountable in terms of personal conduct, performance, and the maintenance of a good company profit margin. They live well-balanced lives. They value integrity within their marriages and their relationships with their children and other family members. They value integrity in the people they work with and exhibit it themselves as they relate to employees, customers, and suppliers. They value and expect integrity in the products and services they deliver to their customers.

For the most part, they have good health and work at keeping it. They experience peace of mind and are content while still eager to contribute more, serve more, and give more. They value friendships and are valued friends. Their focus is on need over greed, service vs. being served, and making their lives count for something.

They have not fallen into the trap of "business as usual" by compromising their ethical standards of conduct for the modern-day, conditional approach to integrity. They know the truth and live it because high ethical standards of conduct have produced multiple dimensions of true profitability—economic wealth, career and company longevity, good personal health, good relationships, and family stability.

By holding true to high ethical standards for conduct, they have kept their lives and their businesses on solid rock. They hold firm to proven standards for conduct regardless of bad situations, personal whims, opportunities for short-term profits, or personal convenience or advantage. My observations support the conclusion that the Judeo-Christian ethical standards for conduct serve as a solid foundation for promoting

- consistent ethical behavior and good performance;
- trust;
- loyalty;
- high levels of motivation;
- high productivity potential;
- excellent economic stability;
- honesty.

People who are consistently productive are firmly committed to personal performance that is firmly based on Judeo-Christian ethical standards for conduct. Those who base their performance on the conditional approach to integrity too often capitulate under pressure and behave in unproductive and often destructive ways.

CONDUCT YOUR OWN COMPARISON TEST

Review the *proven and profitable* leadership traits that follow. Write in front of each trait the degree to which, 1 (low) to 4 (high), you have personally exhibited the bold face traits grounded on Judeo-Christian ethical standards for conduct. How have you experienced them helping you improve your productivity and, if you're employed, your organization's financial reserves?

Also write to the right of each opposing *italicized* trait the degree to which each trait has deterred your success at home and work.

Under each pair, note examples to support your views and discuss them with your family or a trusted colleague.

Accepting-_Contentious_	**Generous-**_Greedy_	**Patient-**_Angry_
Blameless-_Crooked_	**Gracious-**_Profane_	**Peaceful-**_Violent_
Cheerful-_Hot tempered_	**Honest-**_Fraudulent_	**Persevering-**_Idle_
Decisive-_Complacent_	**Hopeful-**_Pessimistic_	**Polite-**_Insulting_
Dignified-_Insolent_	**Humble-**_Arrogant_	**Positive-**_Rebellious_
Diligent-_Lazy_	**Just-**_Unfair_	**Prudent-**_Wasteful_
Discerning-_Careless_	**Kind-**_Cruel_	**Sincere-**_Pretender_
Disciplined-_Unrestrained_	**Loyal-**_Cunning_	**Trustworthy-**_Treacherous_
Discreet-_Brazen_	**Loving-**_Hateful_	**Truthful-**_Liar_
Earnest-_Deceitful_	**Merciful-**_Wicked_	**Understanding-**_Impatient_
Forgiving-_Resentful_	**Open-**_Closed_	**Wise-**_Prideful_

INTENTIONAL INTEGRITY . . .
THE RIGHT PARADIGM

"Total Quality Management" and "Continuous Measurable Improvement" have given us valuable strategies focused on improving productivity and economic success.

The following elements are included in the criteria for the prestigious Malcolm Baldridge National Quality Award. I have described them in terms you can apply to the management of quality in yourself, your family, and your work place.

- *Customer-Driven Quality*—You, your family members, and your colleagues at work should let quality be judged by your "customers." (Spouse, children, employees, consumers.)

- *Leadership*—As a leader at home or elsewhere, you must create a customer orientation.

- *Continuous Improvement*—Achieving the highest level of quality requires a well-defined and well-executed approach to continuous improvement.

- *Employee Participation and Development*—Your organization's (personal life, family, business) success in improving performance depends increasingly on the skills and motivation of those who are part of it and work in it.

- *Fast Response*—Success demands ever-shorter cycles of improvement and service.

- *Design Quality and Prevention*—Place a strong emphasis on design quality and achieve problem and waste prevention through building quality and service into all processes.

- *Long-Range Outlook*—Maintain a strong future orientation and a willingness to make long-term commitments to all stakeholders.

- *Management by Fact*—Build your organization upon a foundation of measurement, data, and analysis rather than opinion.

- *Partnership Development*—Seek to build internal and external partnerships to better accomplish your overall goals.

- *Corporate Responsibility and Citizenship*—Have objectives and ethics that protect public health, public safety, and the environment.

Though the quality and improvement formulas are valuable, I've found two key components weak or missing that need to be in place if quality standards are to pay off consistently and over the long haul: (1) Clear standards for ethical conduct; and (2) Workable performance accountability processes.

I don't want to come across as suggesting you throw the baby (TQM) out with the bath water because the soap isn't effective enough. To the contrary, I urge you to understand and keep the "stuff" of TQM and strengthen it with clear standards for conduct and mutual accountability processes.

A CALL TO CHANGE

I'm proposing that you and I join hands with others who are committed to intentional integrity and who want it to emerge as the new operational paradigm driving America's future. Wouldn't you like to see it embodied by individuals, families, schools, governments, churches, and other institutions throughout the land?

Integrity starts with fathers and mothers in their families and with the board members and top executives in any given organization. When modeled from the top down, integrity has a greater chance of becoming an operational reality among members of the family and among all levels of employees in an organization.

TIME OUT! *Reflect on:*
What? So What? and Now What?

Key Reflections

1. What are the attributes of your character?
2. What are the benefits of being a person of good character?
3. What action steps will you take to be accountable for good conduct?

Part 2

BRINGING YOUR LIFE INTO BALANCE

3

TAKING STOCK:
YOUR WHEEL OF LIFE

For years I've made it an annual practice to revise my written purpose and vision statements. I've also developed mission statements that are tied to my purpose and vision for my family, career, and business. I've reviewed them with my wife and colleagues from time to time so I could have up-to-date written mission statements that help me create a mental picture of where I want to be heading in each dimension of my life.

I've found that my value orientation—worldly or godly—has always determined whether I remained on course or got off course in terms of making a positive contribution toward my life purpose and vision. When I remained focused on the Judeo-Christian ethical standards for conduct my father and mother taught me and modeled for me, I would stay on course and not compromise my integrity. I would think, say, and do the right thing . . . even in difficult times and when my integrity was under fire.

When I capitulated to a conditional approach to integrity, I went astray and did the wrong thing. I rationalized and rationalized . . . ultimately believing many of the "ration of lies" I was telling myself and that others were often telling me.

In time, God's reality prevailed and I realized that the only way I could consistently reach the most valued goals I had established for my life was to behave congruently with the Judeo-Christian ethical standards for conduct I knew were pleasing to God.

I came to this point when I saw that the Judeo-Christian ethical standards for conduct were based on God's principles for living and working found in the Bible. These dependable principles for living life had been set into motion by God and they had definite cause-and-effect outcomes associated with them. Once I understood this, I knew my two basic choices were to obey or decay! I found that if I ignored God's values and principles for living and His laws of cause and effect, I could expect wrong outcomes.

TIME OUT! *Reflect on:*
What? So What? and Now What?

Key Reflections

1. To what core operating values are you committed?
2. How will they make each part of your life more balanced and worthwhile?
3. What do you need to change to align your life with them?

TAKING STOCK OF YOUR WHEEL OF LIFE

In the following chapters of this book, you'll be focusing on how you can strengthen and align certain "spokes" on your Wheel of Life and how you can use key Total Integrity Management tools to help keep your balance in life. The tools will help you keep the various "spokes" or dimensions of your wheel stable and moving along smoothly. You'll find illustrations of possible content for developing each spoke included with the questions for each spoke in appendix A.

If your life is like mine, it sometimes feels as difficult to keep in balance as if you were trying to ride a unicycle. Sometimes life seems to be going too fast or too slow for you to maintain balance. Sometimes you'll experience grinding because you've neglected to lubricate the hub and keep it clean. Sometimes it will show wear and tear on the outer edges because of a misalignment of your spokes. Sometimes it will turn smoothly and get you to where you want to go quickly and easily.

Whether your Wheel of Life is running on the rough side or the smooth side, the fast side or slow side, you can make it stronger and cause it to function better. All it takes is an investment of time in caring for your wheel, aligning the different "spokes," and lubricating the friction points that are causing wear and tear. Pay particular attention to the "spiritual bearings" at the hub of your Wheel of Life.

Wheel of Life

The main "spokes" you'll be examining on your Wheel of Life are the spiritual, physical, emotional, family, recreational, social, financial, community, professional, and intellectual dimensions of your life. You'll be taking stock of each to determine if it is properly aligned with your hub.

Now make a copy of the Wheel of Life, Taking Stock Inventory, score sheet, and profile on the following pages. Put them in your notebook and complete them. Complete the inventory thoughtfully and imagine that someone who really knows you and you trust (your spouse or best friend) is answering each question. This will help you avoid the trap of recording what you want to be instead of accurately assessing how you really are functioning in each dimension of your life.

Wheel of Life: Taking Stock Inventory

Please reflect objectively on each item as you take stock and complete this inventory. The goal is to get an accurate "snapshot" of the relative balance you're presently experiencing between the different dimensions of your life. Weight each item using increments of 5, from 0 to a maximum of 20 points.

To what degree, Low < 0-5-10-15-20 < High, do you . . .

1. ☐ Attend worship services weekly?
2. ☐ Participate in independent and group learning activities?
3. ☐ Maintain an accurate, healthy self-concept?
4. ☐ Engage in a satisfying career or work of your choice?
5. ☐ Involve yourself in community affairs and activities?
6. ☐ Believe you get paid well for your work?
7. ☐ Maintain relationships with a variety of close friends?
8. ☐ Regularly involve yourself in physically active leisure?
9. ☐ Regularly spend quality time with family members?
10. ☐ Exercise vigorously a minimum thirty minutes, three times a week?
11. ☐ Engage in a personal ministry supporting the Great Commission, Matthew 28:19–20?
12. ☐ Listen to educational audiotapes and TV programs?

13. ☐Express positive feelings of love? (patience, kindness, calm understanding, etc.)

14. ☐Recognize and capitalize on unusual career growth opportunities at work?

15. ☐Participate actively in service groups and associations within your community?

16. ☐Participate in an adequate retirement fund?

17. ☐Make friends easily?

18. ☐Enjoy participating in outdoor activities?

19. ☐Regularly communicate with members of your family?

20. ☐Eat nutritious, well-balanced meals?

21. ☐Schedule quiet time daily for prayer and reading the Bible?

22. ☐Go to museums, fairs, and libraries?

23. ☐Problem-solve in conflict situations rather than attack and defend?

24. ☐Demonstrate diligence, joy, and contentment when doing your work?

25. ☐Volunteer for community projects?

26. ☐Maintain a substantial savings program?

27. ☐Enjoy meeting new people?

28. ☐Take spontaneous trips?

29. ☐Enjoy family activities and events?

30. ☐Maintain a lean, well-toned body?

31. ☐Participate in a small-group Bible study and prayer group?

32. ☐Read nonfiction books?

33. ☐Quickly acknowledge and resolve emotions of fear, anger, hurt, and frustration?

34. ☐Assess the impact your character, competence, and commitment has on your career?

35. ☐Initiate community projects?

36. ☐Develop and effectively remain within your budget?

37. ☐Enjoy going to parties and group events?

38. ☐ Take planned trips?

39. ☐ Take time to encourage and support family members in achieving their goals?

40. ☐ Maintain good dental hygiene?

41. ☐ Develop and regularly assess and revise your spiritual growth goals?

42. ☐ Attend classes and seminars?

43. ☐ Nondefensively receive personal feedback and acknowledge mistakes?

44. ☐ Have a career development plan and review it quarterly?

45. ☐ Respond to the call when asked to take community leadership roles?

46. ☐ Control debt and work a plan to become debt-free as soon as possible?

47. ☐ Have a desire to reach out and include new people in social gatherings?

48. ☐ Take "mini vacations" during the week to relax and enjoy people and fun activities?

49. ☐ Hold family accountability and coaching meetings to grow in integrity?

50. ☐ Avoid putting things into or on your body that are likely to harm it?

SCORING AND PLOTTING

Now look at the headings below for each "spoke" or dimension on your Wheel of Life. Record the scores from each numbered item on the inventory you just completed and tally them on the total line under each heading.

Spiritual	Community	Physical	Emotional
1. ☐	5. ☐	10. ☐	3. ☐
11. ☐	15. ☐	20. ☐	13. ☐
21. ☐	25. ☐	30. ☐	23. ☐
31. ☐	35. ☐	40. ☐	33. ☐
41. ☐	45. ☐	50. ☐	43. ☐
Total ☐	Total ☐	Total ☐	Total ☐

Intellectual
2. ☐
12. ☐
22. ☐
32. ☐
42. ☐
Total ☐

Recreational
8. ☐
18. ☐
28. ☐
38. ☐
48. ☐
Total ☐

Social
7. ☐
17. ☐
27. ☐
37. ☐
47. ☐
Total ☐

Career
4. ☐
14. ☐
24. ☐
34. ☐
44. ☐
Total ☐

Financial
6. ☐
16. ☐
26. ☐
36. ☐
46. ☐
Total ☐

Family
9. ☐
19. ☐
29. ☐
39. ☐
49. ☐
Total ☐

After you've tallied the scores for each spoke, plot the score for each spoke on the wheel below by drawing a line across the spoke at the point of the score. Color in each spoke from the hub to the score point with a yellow highlighter.

Your Wheel of Life

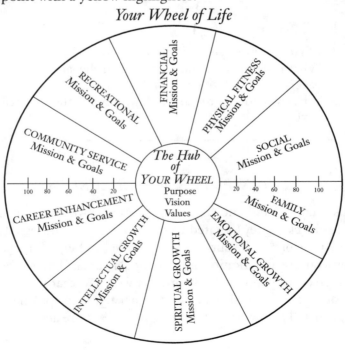

After you've taken stock and completed the assessment portion and filled in the profile of your Wheel of Life with a yellow marker, (1) Reflect on what your wheel might be telling you; and (2) Write in your notebook what you think and feel about the relative balance or imbalance you experience in your life.

Now review the questions listed by number on the Inventory Scoring Sheet related to the different dimensions of your life you want to bring into better balance. Your responses may stimulate insights and ideas that will help you modify, add, or delete some of the things you're thinking, saying, and doing in your life. Remember, the goal is a more balanced life for yourself and the people you relate to in the various dimensions of your life.

TIME OUT! *Reflect on:*
What? So What? and Now What?

Key Reflections

1. What aspects of your life are in and out of balance?
2. What insights have you gained from the survey feedback?
3. What will you do to gain and maintain better balance in your life?

TAKING TIME FOR CHECKUPS

This chapter, and the following chapters, will contain one or more feedback surveys related to the main topics addressed in the particular chapter. The surveys are included to help you take stock of how you are functioning in a particular area. The surveys can also be given to people who know you well and that you trust will give you accurate feedback. By comparing their perspective to yours, you will gain worthwhile insights and a more accurate assessment.

This survey deals with behaviors supportive of intentional integrity. Please take time to complete it and reflect on it.

Personal Intentional Integrity Survey

List the strongest character attributes you exhibit at home.

List the strongest character attributes you exhibit at work.

To what degree (1 low to 10 high) do you function with high integrity at home and work by.

1. ☐ Communicating your life purpose, vision, values, missions, and goals to family members and work colleagues?
2. ☐ Setting and being accountable for high standards of ethical conduct?
3. ☐ Assessing the ethical norms operating at home and work?
4. ☐ Demonstrating ethical leadership practices?
5. ☐ Facilitating the building of an ethical, high-performance family and work team?
6. ☐ Developing ethical relationships between family members and fellow workers?
7. ☐ Communicating truthfully to family members and others?
8. ☐ Taking right action when interpersonal and group dynamics occur?
9. ☐ Resolving conflicts in ethical, mutually productive ways?
10. ☐ Coaching family members and colleagues to enhance one another's "walk and talk" as well as performance?
11. ☐ Demonstrating high integrity managerial practices at home and work?
12. ☐ Participating in a mutual accountability process?
13. ☐ Setting and achieving ethically sound and relevant personal and work goals?
14. ☐ Managing time efficiently and contributing productively?

15. ☐Appraising performance in ways that promote ethical conduct?

16. ☐Supporting ethical marketing practices?

17. ☐Supporting ethical sales practices?

18. ☐Supporting ethical customer service practices?

19. ☐Demonstrating ethical financial practices?

TIME OUT! *Reflect on:*
Your intent to be a person of integrity!

Write for twenty minutes on, "I intend to be a person of integrity by . . . ."

RELAX, ENJOY, LIGHTEN UP . . .

I've never known a person who achieved perfect integrity and balance in his or her life other than our Lord Jesus Christ. I've found life to be in a constant state of flux and change. As soon as my life seems to get close to a sense of balance, things happen and I have to keep working at adjusting over and over again to regain what I feel is *relative equilibrium* or balance. I've found it to be an exciting, rewarding, and constant process of *integrity management!*

Are you committed to diligently and regularly inspecting each dimension of your life to see that it is aligned with your life purpose, supportive of your life vision, and congruent with the biblically-based values you've established for living your life? These are the "bearings" you'll address in the next chapter that give substance to the hub of your wheel.

4

THE HUB:
YOUR KEY TO BALANCE

I currently serve on the board of a local nonprofit group called Todos Hermanos. Todos Hermanos is a newly formed multicultural, charitable and educational community service organization committed to serving at-risk youth and their families in the Newport-Costa Mesa area. We do this through the coordination and delivery of a variety of quality programs in the homes, at schools, and on the streets, by providing linkage among the many community resources available to help at-risk students and their families.

Roy Alvarado is our executive director. Roy is a gang counselor. He received most of his credentials on the streets of Stanton. He saw his brothers attend San Quentin. He was in gangs, took drugs, dealt drugs and was in and out of prison for fourteen years.

While in prison, Roy received training for a career in hairstyling. When he was released, he became one of the most successful hairstylists in town. However, Roy's problems continued. He returned to his old ways and again started taking and pushing drugs. He was arrested and tried. Judge Munoz gave him an alternative—get into a Twelve-Step program or go back to prison for a long time. Roy did not want to go back to prison, so he agreed to the Twelve-Step program.

In this program, Roy started the process of building a spiritual center. He examined his life and developed a heartfelt desire to have a worthwhile purpose. He got the vision of helping prevent young at-risk students from going down the wrong path to drugs, gangs, and crime that he and his brothers had traveled. He took college courses, completed an intern assignment, and became a certified counselor.

Today Roy is retained by our local school district to counsel and run a gang prevention program for at-risk youth in our local high schools. He is successfully guiding "wanna-be" gang members into student leaders with a hope and direction for a worthwhile future. He does drug counseling at local hospitals and for other agencies and started a newsletter for gang counselors. That's what a solid hub will do in a person's life.

Throughout his fight against liver cancer this last year, Roy has exhibited boundless positive energy and a "get it done for the kids" attitude that is contagious. Even after his monthly treatments that wear down his energy and cause blisters in his mouth, he comes to board meetings and conducts business with a display of his usual enthusiasm and energy.

I and others have been praying for Roy. A time came when it looked like the cancer was contained, and we all praised God and celebrated. However, I'm saddened to say it appeared again and Roy's battle with the disease continues.

I count it a great privilege to be working alongside him as a community volunteer. I pray that God will perform a miracle and completely restore Roy's health so that he can have many more years to serve the youth of our community.

THE CENTER OF LIFE

The center of a wheel is the hub. For a wheel to turn freely, it needs a well-designed hub. Our lives, too, must have a "hub," a spiritual center, with well-designed and lubricated main bearings (purpose, vision, values). This is the hub to which we attach "spokes" (the various dimensions of life) to the rim (the integrated whole of the various dimensions of life). The rim transfers the whole of your life through the tire (your character, competence, and commitment) to the road (those around you). The rubber on your tire—your character, competence, and commitment—gives you the ability to travel life's rough roads or smooth trails.

In this chapter you'll have the opportunity to clarify and write your life purpose statement, life vision statement, and the operating values for your life. We'll explore ideas to help you assess, determine, and install your core operating values. These values will support the different dimensions of your life and will become the "stuff" that guides your writing of a vision statement to which you will be accountable. You'll also learn how to evaluate your selected operating values against God's standards.

In addition, we'll examine some "how to" strategies for building boundaries around your life to protect and support your core values. These strategies will help you reduce the risk of compromising your core operating values.

ESTABLISHING YOUR PURPOSE

Webster states that *purpose* is "the object for which anything exists or is done, made, used, etc." Most of the people I meet, even Christians, do not have a clearly defined purpose for their lives. A clear purpose is the first step to achieving true balance in your life—the kind of balance that will bring you lasting joy and peace of mind. The next step is to make a commitment to align all aspects of your life and live them within the parameters of this God-given purpose.

If someone were examining what you've been thinking, saying, and doing, what would they think your purpose in life was? What would they think it was as they looked at your checkbook entries and the events scheduled on your calendar? As they talked to your spouse, children, and business associates? Would their conclusions match what you deeply desire your purpose in life to be? Do you even know what you desire it to be? Do you know what God desires it to be?

A little booklet entitled "Establishing Your Life Purpose" from Vision Ministries helped me see the importance of the last question. "For a Christian, purpose is what God wants his life to add up to and why. The only difference for the nonbeliever is who he is pleasing with his purpose. Purpose is in part gained by understanding the program of God, while your objectives and activities are determined by understanding the role you are to play in participating in that program. If you do not know what God is doing, it is difficult to know how to participate!"[7]

People often limit their thinking about purpose to an occupational or world view. They do not think deeply about their relation to their Creator and the purpose He had in mind for their lives when He created them.

God's view of purpose is the same for every person. God's Word shows us over and over again that He is in the people business. He is calling to Himself a redeemed people to share eternity with Him.

Throughout the Gospels Jesus Christ was asked the meaning and purpose of life, and His answers point to God's universal purpose for our lives.

His purpose for all of us has four aspects:

1. To know God.

   "This is what the LORD says: 'Let not the wise man boast of his wisdom or the strong man boast of his strength or the rich man boast of his riches, but let him who boasts boast about this: that he understands and knows me, that I am the LORD, who exercises kindness, justice and righteousness on earth, for in these I delight,' declares the LORD" (Jer. 9:23–24).

   "But seek first his kingdom and his righteousness, and all these things will be given to you as well" (Matt. 6:33).

2. To become Christlike.

   "For those God foreknew he also predestined to be conformed to the likeness of his Son, that he might be the first-born among many brothers" (Rom. 8:29).

3. To understand the program of God.

   "He made known his ways to Moses, his deeds to the people of Israel" (Ps. 103:7).

4. To become involved in the program of God.

   "Teacher, which is the greatest commandment in the Law?"

   Jesus replied: "'Love the Lord your God with all your heart and with all your soul and with all your mind.' This is the first and greatest commandment. And the second is like it: 'Love your neighbor as yourself.' All the Law and the Prophets hang on these two commandments" (Matt. 22:36–40).

"Therefore go and make disciples of all nations, baptizing them in the name of the Father and of the Son and of the Holy Spirit, and teaching them to obey everything I have commanded you. And surely I am with you always, to the very end of the age" (Matt. 28:19–20).

My Life Purpose Statement

I'm not suggesting my own purpose statement as an ideal model. However, I did think showing it to you would give you an idea of what one looks like after a lot of thinking, praying, and editing! The purpose statement below is at the top of each of the prayer journal pages I use during my daily quiet time with the Lord. I revise it whenever the Spirit moves me.

> My purpose is to be a fully devoted follower of Christ by knowing and loving Him and others; to glorify Him; become Christ-like in what I think, say, and do; to understand His plan; and to participate with Him and others in His plan by evangelizing and discipling men (and with my wife, Barbara, couples) as the Lord puts them before me.

Try writing your own life purpose statement, and include the four components: (1) to know God; (2) to become Christlike; (3) to understand God's program; and (4) to become involved in God's program.

TIME OUT!

Write a draft of your Life Purpose Statement

Now that you have written your purpose statement, are you willing to commit to it? This is where the rubber meets the road in terms of intentional integrity. Is your intent to plan the mission, goals, and objectives for each spoke in your Wheel of Life with your life purpose at the center of the hub? How will you know you are aligning and growing in each aspect of your life in a way that is congruent with your purpose?

Focusing on the purpose God has for your life and His commands will help you achieve worthwhile outcomes in each aspect of your life. Peter focused on this when he said: "For this very reason, make every effort to add to your faith goodness; and to goodness, knowledge; and to knowledge, self-control; and to self-control, perseverance; and to perseverance, godliness; and to godliness, brotherly kindness; and to brotherly kindness, love. For if you possess these qualities in increasing measure, they will keep you from being ineffective and unproductive in your knowledge of our Lord Jesus Christ" (2 Pet. 1:5–8).

Focusing on what God has declared to be good character will give you a satisfying sense of aligning your heart with God as you intentionally live out His value system. This focus will produce increasing contentment and balance in each aspect of your life. This focus will give you a stronger and clearer sense of how dependent you are upon God for everything, including the establishing of your mission, goals, and objectives for each spoke on your Wheel of Life.

ESTABLISHING YOUR LIFE VISION

Your *universal purpose* is why you exist. You were made by and are used by God to carry out His plan. Your life vision is what you uniquely *can be and do* on a particular "playing field." This "playing field" is where your natural God-given talents, interests, and motivations can harmoniously come together. It's where you can make highly productive contributions to your own well-being, that of your family, and others around you.

To get a taste of what a vision is like, think about a mental picture you've had in the past . . . like owning your own bed and breakfast establishment on a lake in the mountains. Think about what you wanted your first home to look and be like, your career, a special vacation, your children's future. How did having a clear picture in your mind impact your motivation to make one or more of these pictures or visions a reality? How did having this clear picture in your mind impact your commitment to work toward your vision becoming a reality?

God created in our brains a wonderful mechanism called the reticular activating system. It is found in a section near the lower back portion of the brain. It helps us bring to consciousness those things we need to achieve our vision.

Here's how it works in day-to-day necessities. As my son, grandsons, and I drive down the highway, we're talking and laughing over the fish stories of the past. I'm enjoying the family and could not tell you how many gas stations we've passed along Highway 395.

When I notice the gas gauge at a low point, my reticular activating system goes into play. It starts scanning the environment not only for gas stations, but for Shell gas stations, because that is the only credit card I have!

The reticular activating system operates the same way when we have a worthwhile, God-honoring, "can and should be" vision for our lives. It draws our attention to the right things at the right time to lead us toward the achievement of our vision.

Think about Proverbs 29:18 in the King James Version, "Where there is no vision, the people perish: but he that keepeth the law, happy is he." Doesn't this highlight the importance of having a clear, worthwhile vision of a life of intentional integrity?

Your vision statement for your life may end up being long or short, written in paragraphs or in outline form. Some people prefer to limit it to a slogan. The important thing is to *have one* and review it frequently so that your reticular activating system will focus on what you need to do to make it a reality.

My Life Vision Statement

"The vision I have for my life is one of unselfishly serving others and functioning competently and excellently as a husband, father, grandfather, friend, business consultant, educator, and author. I am committed to God to hold myself accountable and encourage my wife, children, clients, and others to hold me accountable, for being of good character and thinking, saying, and doing the righteous thing in all situations."

TIME OUT!
Write a draft of your Life Vision Statement.

ESTABLISHING YOUR LIFE OPERATING VALUES

Again, the universal life purpose statement you've developed should communicate why you exist and how you are used by God as His creation. The life vision statement you've developed should communicate what you uniquely *can be and do* on a particular "playing field" of life that allows you to effectively carry out your purpose in a way pleasing to God.

Now we'll examine how your operating values relate to the above. One definition *Webster's* gives for the word *value* is, "that property of a thing because of which it is esteemed, desirable, or useful, or the degree of this property possessed; worth, merit, or importance." I'm using this definition as we discuss your personal operating values, those values you hold as having worth, merit, and importance for being a "property" of yourself and that guide you in the way you operate or behave at home and work.

Your core operating values should be those you want to motivate your decisions, conduct, and commitments while in the process of *achieving* and *expediting* your purpose and vision.

All people have professed, expressed, and impressed values. Professed values are those values we tell people we stand for or put in "We believe" statements, credos, or vision statements. Expressed values are those we live out and express behaviorally. Impressed values are those that have captured our heads and hearts and often compete internally to replace some older, conflicting values we've held on to in the past.

Most often, people trust and respect us when our professed values and expressed values are congruent—when we're "walking the walk and walking our talk." That's why it is important to intentionally select the operating values we desire to manifest in action.

Which came first, vision or values? The fact is our life operating values are often imbedded in our life vision statements. In my case, the values I've grown to hold dear have dictated a great deal of my life vision. In any case, it is important to keep your life operating values clearly in view. I selected a number of mine from the specifics Paul laid out when he talked about the excellence of love in 1 Corinthians 13. After I made a list of my life operating values for the hub of my own Wheel of Life, I turned them into an accountability survey that I complete and have my wife, Barbara, complete for me from time to time. This feedback helps me keep clear on the values I intend to live by and pulls me up short when my walk and talk are not congruent.

The Bible is *the best source* for finding worthwhile operating values that will guide you toward righteousness and a balanced life. Read it and pick the values most important to you along with those that will help strengthen your character.

My Values Check

During the past week, to what degree (1 low to 10 high) have I honored God through my life operating values by

1. ☐ Demonstrating fidelity in relationship to my wife, children, colleagues, and clients?

2. ☐ Demonstrating patience in doing work and interacting with people?

3. ☐ Expressing kindness toward all persons?

4. ☐ Showing gratitude at home and work?

5. ☐ Demonstrating graciousness in dealing with people?

6. ☐ Serving my family, colleagues and others with a humble spirit?

7. ☐ Demonstrating politeness in word and deed?

8. ☐ Regularly giving to others?

9. ☐ Expressing calm understanding in dealing with conflict?

10. ☐ Showing delight in promoting justice?

11. ☐Being honest by telling the truth and taking only what was rightfully mine?

12. ☐Reaching out to forgive mistakes and faults?

13. ☐Showing trust in others?

14. ☐Demonstrating hope in difficult situations?

15. ☐Demonstrating loyalty to others?

16. ☐Showing perseverance in achieving results?

17. ☐Manifesting good will in word and deed?

FINAL THOUGHTS ABOUT PURPOSE, VISION, AND VALUES

Over the years I've been diligent about developing, maintaining, and "lubricating" the bearings in the hub of my own Wheel of Life—my Life Purpose, my Life Vision, and my Life Operating Values. Investing a block of time each month to examine, maintain, and repair these three bearings has helped me to build and enjoy a life that has increasingly become more loving, easygoing, fruitful, fulfilling, and peaceful.

Looking back over the years, I see that the operating values I've established for myself can be likened to fence posts I've put deep into the ground. On these posts I've constructed rails to keep me from straying too far off course from my purpose, vision and values.

I've found the notion of using my value posts as the foundation points for constructing important boundaries in my life an important one. These boundaries have helped me focus on being a person of intentional integrity.

I'm not going to discuss the details of boundary building with you, but instead encourage you to read a great book on the subject. The book is *Boundaries: When to Say Yes, When to Say No to Take Care of Your Life* by Dr. Henry Cloud and Dr. John Townsend. It is full of practical strategies and principles for building the boundaries you need and want in your life. Read it and you'll have additional tools to help you achieve the balance you desire.

In closing this chapter, I want to share with you what God tells us is a vitally important value post for the health and preservation of marriage and family. It is the value post of fidelity. As a result of putting this post deep in the ground, I've been faithfully married to and have loved my wife, Barbara, since 1951.

I'm not sharing this for pride's sake but with humility and gratitude. I'm grateful that my mother and father, through God's grace, helped me develop this value post at an early age.

My mom raised goats because I needed goat's milk. I was a premature baby with digestive problems. Can you imagine many professional mothers, like my mom who was a graduate nurse, taking the initiative to raise and milk goats to help nurture their children?

Mom used our family of goats to teach me the value of human fidelity. She built upon the awesome experiences of watching and helping with the birth of the kid goats each year. She explained how dependent each newborn child is on a good and loving mother and father. She taught me that it was a serious matter to decide to bring a baby into this world. She taught me the importance of nurture and care. I listened and learned and valued what she taught me.

Mom and Dad also taught me about the dangers of sexually transmitted diseases and how your health can be ruined for life if you contract a disease through sex outside of marriage.

As a result of my parents' teaching and example, I put the fidelity value post deep into the ground. This post has helped me honor the values I established at an early age and to stay inside those boundaries. It helped to keep strong temptations from breaking through and kept me from breaking out. It has been a blessing to me and to Barbara, as well as our three children and grandchildren, who have benefited from knowing and observing us as we've lived the value of fidelity during a lifetime.

A surprising reward came as a result of honoring this operating value of fidelity. In the summer of 1994, our son, Scott, married a wonderful woman, Laura, who we love like one of our own daughters. Scott asked me to be his best man. I continue to savor the honor and pleasure of it.

The printed wedding program was an unusually beautiful fourteen-page booklet filled with heart-touching thoughts from the bride and groom to all twenty-four of their attendants! Along with other things, the program contained a message from Laura and Scott to their parents.

Scott wrote to Barbara and me . . .

> Dear Mom and Dad,
>
> I know there's a sigh of relief that you've finally got this last one married off! I can just hear it now, "The girls were easy . . . but Scott, he might be a bit of a challenge." No worries, I was just waiting for Laura to come into my life—she's often late, you know.
>
> I love you both very much! I'm not sure why God chose two parents as loving, giving, and supportive as you two for me; but whatever the reason is, I'm glad He did. I've often told people throughout the years that there is no one or nothing in this world that I have enough faith in, that I would stake my life on, except your marriage.
>
> I have had the privilege of watching over my lifetime a relationship that is truly built on a phrase which is used much too lightly these days—"unconditional love." What I bring into this marriage with Laura is built by you two. You have given me a wedding gift that has been nurtured over the past thirty years, and compares to no other gift that could be given today . . . role models for marriage.
>
> Thank you for your love, Scott.

Scott wrote to me as his best man . . .

> You're a tough act to follow. I only hope to be as great a father to my children as you have been to me. You never hesitated to tell me you love me, give me a hug, tell me how proud and lucky you are to have a son like me, to spend time with me, or tell me that I might be making a mistake. All that you said to me was always heard and is still felt. I've always respected your honesty, morals, and sense of humor. Though sometimes I couldn't find the emotions or words to return back to you, I want you to know that I do love you very much and you always have been and truly are my best man.

By God's grace, it is never too late to establish righteous values for our lives. However, the earlier, the better. If you haven't thought through and established the values to guide your life, now is the time to get clear on what they are, what they should be by God's standards, and what you desire for them to be.

My hope and prayer is that you feel motivated to take the time to carefully think through and develop with great seriousness your own core operating values. I promise that the fulfillment of your life purpose and vision will come to fruition more easily and quickly if you do. You will also be positioning yourself as a model of "values in action" if you have children. And what a blessing they will be to you as you grow older!

TIME OUT!
Develop your main list of Life Operating Values.

5

DEVELOPING SPIRIT-DRIVEN MISSIONS, GOALS, AND OBJECTIVES FOR YOUR SPOKES

A few years ago I became a regular participant in a local Christian Business Men's Committee. Our weekly gathering included a small group meeting for prayer, a wonderful and tasty Friday morning breakfast, good fellowship, and a program of someone's testimony or a short Bible study. We were a very comfortable and congenial group of Christians.

What I didn't know until Craig Kiggens came to southern California as a CBMC staff man, was that what we were doing at our meetings wasn't all that CBMC was about. As we learned more from Craig about the mission and expectations of CBMC, our numbers decreased. Over a short time, we ended up with only five men!

As we sought God's guidance, He made it clear to us that we each needed to focus on our own spiritual growth and establish for ourselves spiritual growth goals.

We started by forming a weekly prayer and support group. As we attempted to develop our own spiritual growth goals, we did it with a considerable amount of resistance, procrastination, and avoidance. We found that looking forthrightly at our own sins and making a commitment to God and to each other to grow in His likeness was no easy task.

After two years, the five prayer warriors were in a position to help get a renewed committee on the right footing. The committee began to grow in number as members reached out to bring nonbelieving men to outreach testimonies and then followed through by discipling them. We linked them with spiritual growth programs that CBMC, churches, and other ministries sponsored in Orange County.

What I took away from this sojourn was a deep respect for the growth power that came from having spiritual growth goals in place and making them a top priority in my life. I now find myself more often than not blessed and filled with Christ's loving patience and calm understanding, even in the heat of conflict. Believe me, this is not my nature! I believe my ability to "let go and let God" fill me with His patience and calm understanding has been one of the results of having clearly written spiritual growth goals and diligently maintaining a regular prayer and Bible study time each day. This is why I believe the spiritual growth spoke is the most important spoke on a person's Wheel of Life.

Over the years, I've come to realize that this spoke needs to be continually "trued" to the hub and rim of my Wheel of Life as I travel down life's road. When a bicycle wheel is out of balance, it is "trued." Each spoke is tightened just right so that the wheel doesn't wobble. Truing—both the word and the process—is an excellent metaphor for living a life of intentional integrity.

My spiritual spoke is made up of my prayerfully determined spiritual growth mission, goals and objectives. As you work your way through this book, you'll see how important it is to consistently attend to the "truing" of this spoke so that it doesn't become too loose and cause your Wheel of Life to get out of true.

DEVELOPING YOUR SPIRITUAL GROWTH GOALS

In the past, I confused spiritual growth with religious activities. I later learned it was more important to have, and work at achieving, specific spiritual growth goals instead of just participating in religious activities. The verses that help me keep focused on spiritual growth are:

"Be perfect, therefore, as your heavenly Father is perfect" (Matt. 5:48).

"As for God, his way is perfect; the word of the LORD is flawless. He is a shield for all who take refuge in him" (2 Sam. 22:31).

"If you love me, you will obey what I command" (John 14:15).

With this insight, I was able to write clearer goals and then list the measurable objectives or supporting activities that were the most relevant to achieving my goals.

The process for mission development, goal-setting, and objective-listing has worked well for me. I've shared it with my accountability group partners, my children, my Bible study group members, and my clients. Those who have taken the time to diligently implement the process as part of their regular life and business planning efforts have more easily, quickly, and consistently achieved worthwhile results.

INVESTING TIME IN THE PROCESS

This process for developing your missions, goals, and objectives will work wonders for you as you "true" your Wheel of Life by tightening up your "loose" spokes. The key is to discipline yourself and keep coming back to this section *until you are sure you understand it.*

Implementing the process of tightening your spokes and truing your wheel requires *a serious and regular investment of your time.* You may want to find a quiet place to work on this. Be open and sensitive to seeking God's will as you work on each spoke.

Begin with a commitment to engage in the process for a minimum of thirty days. After thirty days evaluate your progress. Most likely you'll have begun to experience incrementally the benefits from beginning to bring balance to your life and will want to continue the process and refine it to fit your style. Keep working on refining the goal-setting process for yourself. Talk to other people who are diligently setting and achieving goals. Read books on the subject. Keep practicing and refining the process until you establish, evaluate, and revise the *worthwhile mission, goals, and objectives* that will guide you as you begin the process of strengthening and balancing all dimensions of your life.

THE PROCESS

The first step is to find quiet time to do some open-ended writing. I write continuously for at least twenty minutes in a nonstop fashion. I keep on writing, even when the words appear to make little sense or fail to have the right flow, proper structure, or spelling.

I ask myself four general questions I can easily make specific to any particular dimension of my life.

1. What's God calling me to do right now?
2. What blocks me from doing it?
3. What do I need to do to remove the blocks?
4. What do I need to do to more consistently think, say, and do what's right to get the right results in my life?

To make the questions more specific, ask, "What's God calling me to do right now *related to family?*" You can substitute the words *finance, recreation, community service, career, intellectual growth, spiritual growth, emotional growth, social activities,* or *physical fitness* to continue your evaluation.

I spend a minimum of twenty minutes of uninterrupted writing on one question at a time. Rushing the process can keep you from getting solid insights. I find the process more fruitful if I focus on being relaxed and allow time between writing on each question. I've found that this writing process is another way of discovering what God is saying to me; and for me that always requires patience, calmness, and quiet.

After I've completed my writing on each question, I take time to study and analyze what I've written. I pray for insight into what I've written and read Scripture relevant to the topics or issues that surface from my writing. I try to cull as much meaning as possible from what I've written. Sometimes I use different colored pens to highlight key words and insights. I also make notes in the margins and formulate questions to myself.

WHERE TO START

The process of bringing balance to your life has to begin someplace. I suggest that you begin with the two significant spokes: spiritual growth and career enhancement. We'll focus on these spokes in this chapter.

I urge you to take time to "tighten" an additional spoke each time you complete a chapter. Questions for each spoke are in appendix A. Select each additional spoke in the order you believe it needs the most attention.

Each time you start to work on another spoke, focus first on the four "big picture" questions and restate them to address the specific spoke you're working on

Following are some additional questions to help you think through what you want to include in the mission, goals, and objectives for the Spiritual Growth Spoke. Make a copy of the questions and keep it available in your journal as you focus on developing your mission, goals, and objectives for this dimension of your life.

1. What will spiritual fulfillment look like from my perspective? Is it compatible with God's perspective?

2. What types of spiritual objectives and activities will help me mature in Christ?

3. What can I do to develop and broaden my worthwhile spiritual activities?

4. What steps do I need to take to accomplish the spiritual objectives I've identified?

5. How will I know my spiritual objectives and activities are contributing to a more balanced, bountiful, and beneficial life according to God's standards?

6. How will I know that my spiritual objectives and activities are the highest and best use of the emotional, physical, time, and financial reserves God has given to me?

When I've completed the questions, I take the second step and begin drafting my mission statement for a particular spoke. A mission statement includes a description of who does what, in relationship to whom, and how it is to be done.

My spiritual growth mission statement reads: "My Spiritual Growth Mission is to intentionally obey God's Word and become a fully devoted follower of Christ as I grow in knowing and loving Him and others through His grace." (The "who" part of this mission statement is *me*. The "does what with whom" portion is *obey God's Word and become a fully devoted follower of Christ*.)

After I've completed my mission statement, I list one to three spiritual growth goals along with the objectives or activities that will help me achieve each goal.

One of my present Spiritual Growth Goals related to my mission is: "To appropriate the loving character of Jesus Christ that He gave me through grace so that I more consistently express His love through my behavior at home and in the marketplace, particularly in the areas of acceptance, patience, and calm understanding."

My enabling objectives/activities for achieving this goal are:

1. Read and study God's Word daily to help me trust, through faith, in His redemption.

2. Take quiet time for prayer each morning and pray throughout the day for an attitude and actions that demonstrate acceptance, patience, and calm understanding.

3. Reflect on answers to prayer and diligently act to do His will in my daily life.

4. Share my goal with my PACT (Performance Accountability Commitment Team) members and report to them weekly on my successes and obstacles. Also ask for personal feedback, coaching, support, and prayer.

5. Request and receive weekly counsel, encouragement, prayer, and personal feedback from Barbara to help me more consistently express Christ's loving nature at home.

6. Take time out as immediately as possible to pray for His character and nature to take over in relationships or situations where I experience reactive, negative emotions.

CAREER ENHANCEMENT SPOKE

Now that you've taken a first cut at "tightening" your spiritual growth spoke by establishing your spiritual growth mission, goals, and objectives, you're ready to continue the process with the center spoke. For many people their career and work are often seriously out of "true" with their spiritual spoke and their Wheel of Life. When people focus too much on their work, they often find it has eaten up their emotional, physical, time, and financial reserves.

TAKE A "WHEEL TRUING" TIME OUT!

Develop a Mission, Goals, and Objectives for Your Spiritual Growth Spoke.

Key Points
1. Write on the "Big Four" questions to get a broad picture.
2. Outline and then write a draft of your mission statement.
3. Develop your goals and list them along with your objectives.

They have little or nothing left for the other dimensions of their out-of-balance lives.

There is a transformation in the wind, and business environments are being restructured or reengineered all over our country. At the same time, people are becoming aware of a deep personal need for meaning. This is creating a work force where many more people than ever before are trying to fill that need for meaning at work. They expect increased satisfaction from work—more than just the paycheck that puts food on the table with something left over for investment and pleasure.

Increasing numbers of people want to work to live, not live to work! They want to be involved in setting worthwhile goals and having input into the way business is conducted. At the same time, they want to gain a sense of meaning and purpose by filling a position that provides them with an opportunity to make genuine contributions to others through the work they do. They want dignity. They want significant relationships with their fellow workers, managers, and customers.

If you are seeking meaning and purpose from the work you do, you may not feel you're getting it on a sustained basis. This could be because you, like many others around you, are operating from a world view rather than a biblical view of your life's purpose and God's purposes for work.

People who have an integrated, balanced set of goals for each dimension of their lives have a unified life purpose. They also have a life vision and a clear set of spiritually driven operating values. They find joy and meaning when they achieve the goals they've set for their careers as well as the other dimensions of their lives.

These people have developed their work goals with an eye on biblical principles, such as examples referred to below. God has given us these principles to help us live the work portion of our lives in a balanced way.

1. *You cannot serve two masters.* God will supply all your needs. "No one can serve two masters. Either he will hate the one and love the other, or he will be devoted to the one and despise the other. You cannot serve both God and Money. Therefore I tell you, do not worry about your life, what you will eat or drink; or about your body, what you will wear. Is not life more important than food, and the body more important than clothes?" (Matt. 6:24–25).

2. *Keep eternity foremost in your mind when doing work.* "I know that there is nothing better for men than to be happy and do good while they live. That everyone may eat and drink, and find satisfaction in all his toil—this is the gift of God. I know that everything God does will endure forever; nothing can be added to it and nothing taken from it. God does it so that men will revere Him. Whatever is has already been, and what will be has been before; and God will call the past to account" (Eccles. 3:12–15).

3. *Enjoy all your labor during the few years God has given you.* "Then I realized that it is good and proper for a man to eat and drink, and to find satisfaction in his toilsome labor under the sun during the few days of life God has given him—for this is his lot. Moreover, when God gives any man wealth and possessions, and enables him to enjoy them, to accept his lot and be happy in his work—this is a gift of God" (Eccles. 5:18–19).

4. *If you don't work, you don't eat.* "For even when we were with you, we gave you this rule: 'If a man will not work, he shall not eat.' We hear that some among you are idle. They are not

busy; they are busybodies. Such people we command and urge in the Lord Jesus Christ to settle down and earn the bread they eat" (2 Thess. 3:10–12).

5. *Cultivate and keep things in good shape.* "The LORD God took the man and put him in the Garden of Eden to work it and take care of it" (Gen. 2:15).

6. *Understand that the fruits of your labor may fail to satisfy you in the long run.* They may often be painful and cause you grief in the short run. They may cause your mind unrest at night. However, God tells us that labor itself is good!

> I hated all the things I had toiled for under the sun, because I must leave them to the one who comes after me. And who knows whether he will be a wise man or a fool? Yet he will have control over all the work into which I have poured my effort and skill under the sun. This too is meaningless. So my heart began to despair over all my toilsome labor under the sun. For a man may do his work with wisdom, knowledge and skill, and then he must leave all he owns to someone who has not worked for it. This too is meaningless and a great misfortune. What does a man get for all the toil and anxious striving with which he labors under the sun? All his days his work is pain and grief; even at night his mind does not rest. This too is meaningless. A man can do nothing better than to eat and drink and find satisfaction in his work. This too, I see, is from the hand of God (Eccles. 2:18–24).

When I develop my goals *and* keep biblical principles like these in mind, I more quickly and easily achieve the goals I've set for all areas of my life. I've observed that this is true for others, too.

Another thing I've observed is that people have increased levels of commitment to achieving their work goals when they are part of a healthy, values-driven organizational culture. In this kind of culture all stakeholders are able to clearly identify and communicate to one another about

1. A vision that is pleasing to God,

2. A set of operating values that are congruent with biblical principles,

3. A worthwhile mission supported by relevant goals and measurable objectives,

4. Their performance expectations and values about service-oriented leadership behaviors such as those described and implied in 1 Corinthians 13,

5. The elements of an organization-wide, mutual accountability process that regularly engages people in coaching one another in the strengthening of character, competence, and commitment.

Are you presently working in this type of organizational environment? If not, are you motivated to take the leadership initiative necessary, with God's help, to begin enhancing it? If not, maybe it is time for you to seriously consider moving to another arena in the marketplace where you can bear greater fruit and achieve greater balance!

Peak-performing, goal-achieving executives, managers, and employees more often than not are persons who engage in thoughtful planning and goal-setting for themselves as well as for their organizations.

Effective planning will always contribute to increasing your important emotional, physical, time, and financial reserves.

Some people spend less time taking care of their lives than they do their expensive cars. Like a well-running car, a well-running balanced life can bring us excitement, pleasure, and satisfaction. Both require regular diagnosis and service, and on some occasions, repairs and new parts.

I've found that peak performers have:

1. Developed their life purpose in terms of God's commands and have conceptualized and written down their life purpose, vision, operating values, mission, goals, and enabling objectives, not just thought about them.

2. Shared the above with their spouses and other family members as well as trusted colleagues at work. They have asked these people for feedback regarding achievement indicators and suggestions for improvement.

3. Used a variety of strategies to review their goals and reinforce their successes along the way to achieving them on a regular basis. They also keep their goals visible in a variety of ways.

Some include them in their calendar books, maintain them on their computers, put them in the front of their Bibles, keep them in notebooks, or record them on audio tapes to play while traveling to and from work.

INVESTING YOUR TIME AND YOUR LIFE IN YOUR WORK WISELY

World-class performers and integrity champions are careful about where they work and with whom they work. They are in high demand and rarely out of work. They seek employment in organizations that have either (1) recruited them because of their demonstrated character, competence, and commitment; or (2) have a high integrity profile as an organization and a substantively healthy organizational culture that attracted them to seek a position.

These attractive, high-integrity and healthy organizations are more often than not led by people who have diligently developed a financially lean and ethically clean organization. They have done it by establishing a culture that supports employees of high character, competence, and commitment. These enterprises enjoy high customer loyalty, good long-term profits, low turnover and absenteeism, and high morale because of management's focus on quality, integrity, and accountability.

Doesn't it make sense to be a good steward of your talents and invest them wisely rather than spend them wastefully during the hours you work? Is where you work now giving you a reasonable opportunity to make a genuine contribution and to grow in character and competence while you receive fair financial compensation?

Following are some additional questions to help you think through what you want to include in the mission, goals, and objectives for the Career Enhancement Spoke attached to the hub of your Wheel of Life. Make a copy of the questions and keep it available in your journal while you are focused on developing your mission, goals, and objectives for this dimension of your life.

Take a "Wheel Truing" Time Out!:
Using the process outlined earlier . . .

Develop a Mission, Goals, and Objectives for Your Career Enhancement Spoke.

Key Points
1. What kind of balance do I have between work and other parts of my life?
2. What are the benefits of having my spiritual and career goals compatible?
3. What is God leading me to change regarding my work?

1. What will career and work fulfillment look like from my perspective? Is it compatible with God's perspective?
2. What types of career objectives and activities will help me mature in Christ?
3. What can I do to develop and broaden my worthwhile career activities?
4. What steps do I need to take to accomplish the career objectives I've identified?
5. How will I know my career objectives and activities are contributing to a more balanced, bountiful, and beneficial life for me according to God's standards?
6. How will I know that my career objectives and activities are the highest and best use of the emotional, physical, time, and financial reserves God has given to me?

Conducting a Regular Maintenance Check

Each time you formulate a new mission, goal or objective to tighten one of the spokes on your Wheel of Life, take time to check if it is trued properly with the hub of your wheel and that the spoke is not causing your wheel to wobble. Make sure that everything is congruent with your purpose, values, and vision as well as in accord and harmony with the Spiritual Growth Spoke of your Wheel of Life. This is also important when you go back to add, delete, or modify things from any of your missions, goals, or objectives.

One of the easiest, quickest, and best ways I've found for truing my wheel as I tighten my different spokes is to share with my wife and with one or more of my PACT partners the specifics of how I'm tightening them. Since I know in advance that I'm going to do this, I find myself carefully checking my mission and goal statements as I finish them. I want to make sure they are not in any way in conflict with my written purpose, values, and vision.

TIME OUT!
Establish your "maintenance check" plan.

Put the "check" points on your calendar!

Key Reflections

1. Are my mission and goal statements in line with my Hub?
2. Are they compatible with the mission and goals of other spokes?
3. Have I checked them out with my spouse or accountability partner?

By now you are well on your way to establishing a mission statement, goals, and objectives for your spiritual growth spoke and your career enhancement spoke. As we shift gears and begin to focus on integrity management skills, you'll have the opportunity to true the other spokes in Time Out activities in upcoming chapters. Refer to this chapter and to appendix A to help you continue the truing process.

Part 3

SEVEN SETS OF PERSONAL INTEGRITY MANAGEMENT SKILLS

6

FOLLOWER SKILLS

Jesus Christ is our perfect example of a proactive, servant leader. He was both the flawless follower and the leader of leaders. He was a follower first and a leader second. He gave Himself totally to following His Father's directions at all times.

THE IMPORTANCE OF BEING AN EFFECTIVE FOLLOWER

How many children, parents, teachers, pastors, and executives are breaking down the door to learn to be excellent followers? Regretfully, I didn't either during the first five decades of my life.

Then I discovered the principle that if I don't attract followers, I can't serve and guide them as a leader. I can't inspire and influence the people around me if they are not *willing* and *able* to follow me. The opposite is also true. I can't be led or inspired if I'm not willing to follow someone else's lead.

I learned a lot about following several years ago when I made a series of bad investment decisions. Every one of the investments looked good on the surface. I was enamored by the apparent intelligence and character of the people advising me. I had started and developed a successful business, saved well, and was ready to increase the assets Barbara and I had saved.

As I invested in a number of limited partnerships, I did not accept Barbara's advice. She seemed overly cautious and too financially conservative. I would not give in to her concerns as I made investment decisions regarding *our* savings. I tried to convince her of the "great opportunity" and safety each investment represented. She was uncomfortable with each of them; she just had a "gut feeling" that it was wrong.

Every one of the investments she questioned failed! What I learned from these costly decisions is never to invest unless there is 100 percent consensus between my wife and myself, regardless of the advice of "expert financial advisors." Now we share the financial leadership responsibility for our family. Each of us leads and follows according to the gifts and talents God has given us. It is easy for both of us to accept leader and follower roles, and we use 100 percent consensus in making all financial decisions.

TEN HALLMARKS OF EFFECTIVE FOLLOWERS

High-integrity followers possess and regularly practice ten important traits. As you set goals for developing these hallmarks as a follower, you'll position yourself to be a more excellent leader when your leadership is called for. You will be the type of leader who provides extraordinary leadership in given situations or in every situation, if you hold a formal position of leadership. You'll make the lives of everyone around you easier because of your capacity to alternate between leading and following when the situation calls for it. Here are the ten hallmarks of a high-integrity follower.[8]

1. *You manage yourself well.* You're on course as you negotiate life's trails because you think for yourself. You are able to exercise control and independence and do the right things without close supervision. People can safely delegate responsibility to you

because you anticipate needs and respond to them appropriately according to your level of competence and authority.

You see yourself as an equal of those you follow and are willing to advocate other positions or views without feeling intimidated by hierarchy and organizational structure. You also recognize that all people in organizations are in a variety of lead-follow relationships that focus on achieving the organization's worthwhile goals.

Unlike ineffective followers, you'll recognize when you are veering off course and becoming ineffective in self-management or if your integrity is beginning to disintegrate as "the system" prompts you to capitulate your values, compromise your character, and fake your competency levels.

You'll recognize when you start to manipulate leaders for your own selfish purposes. You'll take the initiative to keep your false fear of powerlessness from becoming a self-fulfilling prophecy. You do not let your feelings of resentment lead you to undermine your organization's legitimate and worthwhile goals.

2. *You're committed and loyal to your organization.* You like working with others whose hearts are in their work and you help keep morale high. You help keep things on track and on time. As an effective follower you temper your loyalties to satisfy the organization's needs. You know how to direct your energies in ways that satisfy the organization's goals as well as your own personal needs.

Unlike ineffective followers, you do not strongly commit to goals that are inconsistent with the worthwhile goals of your organization. You do not produce destructive results that cause the legitimate leaders in your organization to lose control of it.

3. *You respect the legitimate authority of others.* Your follower skills most often place you in a favored position in relation to others in legitimate authority and your organization's hierarchy. As a self-confident follower, you see colleagues as allies and people in positions of legitimate authority as equal partners as you achieve together your organization's vision, mission, and goals.

You know that the person filling the leadership position has been put there through a legitimate process. You know that it is a follower's position to which you are clearly assigned.

Unlike ineffective followers, you diligently respond to legitimate authority by honoring the position, not necessarily the person. You submit to their direction rather than resist it, even when you don't agree with it and have advocated other courses of action. When you suffer unfair treatment and your leader violates the standards for conduct established by your organization, rather than return ill for ill you earnestly try to think, say, and do the right thing.

4. *You seek specific directions.* You talk with the person to whom you are accountable when you do not know what to do to fulfill your responsibilities. You know how to ask for clear directions to do the job effectively. You also listen attentively when the person in authority gives directions and check to see that you share a common understanding.

Unlike ineffective followers, you never avoid or reject direct orders. You're never afraid to admit you are unsure to your leader or go off talking about your concerns to everyone except your leader. You never seek directions as a ploy to escape your responsibility, and you don't take issue instead of notes when instructions are given to you.

5. *You accept significant assignments.* You do not play it safe. You are willing to risk taking on assignments that many people in the work-place would avoid. You do this because you have an accurate view of your leader and an accurate view of yourself. You take on extra work gladly, but only after doing a superior job of fulfilling your basic responsibilities. You are always well prepared, available, and have a clear understanding of the task. You also value the intrinsic rewards more than the extrinsic rewards you'll receive.

Unlike ineffective followers, you are not afraid of losing your job or personal regard by accepting difficult assignments. As a follower, you do not dodge delegation or muddle around in mediocrity; instead you deliver the goods responsibly.

6. *You develop your competencies and are credible.* You master new skills that will serve your organization and enhance your career options. You regularly invest time and money to enhance your performance by attending training and professional development programs you have sought out.

Unlike ineffective followers, you don't expect training and development to come to you—only going to seminars when sent by your leader. The improvement of your competence and the avoidance of skill deterioration does not depend on your leader taking the responsibility to give you special care and attention.

7. *You focus your efforts for maximum impact.* You expect your organization's performance standards to be legitimately set by your leader. You want them imposed on everyone fairly but at the same time allow for the recognition of excellence that stimulates advancement. You have higher personal performance standards than your organization's culture requires or expects. You are a good judge of your own strengths, and when asked to do things you are poorly qualified to do, you recommend others who are more qualified.

Unlike ineffective followers, you are willing to stretch and don't mind chancing failure if you believe you can succeed. However, you don't want to subtract from your organization's financial reserves by wasting time and energy.

8. *You value honest appraisals and feedback.* You clearly see the wisdom of seeking honest appraisals. You know that whatever you have committed to evaluating you have ended up cultivating. You value honest appraisals and praise the leader who takes the time to provide you with valuable affirmative and corrective feedback. You look forward to informal performance appraisals delivered at unexpected times, because you know there is the possibility that your performance may be less than what is expected or desired by others. You look forward to the process because you know it will enhance your contributions and career success.

Unlike ineffective followers, you actively participate in, rather than submit to or aggressively resist, the performance appraisal process. You never enter into a passive-aggressive conspiracy to block the process when it goes poorly; instead you share with others the benefits you've gained from honest appraisals and feedback from family members, peers, subordinates, and bosses.

9. *You exhibit exemplary integrity and honesty.* You are a person who can be left alone without the risk that you'll take wrong action and create wrong results. Your ethical standards for conduct are based on the proven principles of right behavior found in the Bible. You consistently manifest them in your day-to-day conduct. You know what is legal and abide by it; you know what is possible and ethical and you do it. You pass the "reasonable person" test every time.

TIME OUT! *Reflect on your strengths regarding each hallmark.*

Make copies of the following survey and put at least one copy in your notebook for each dimension of your life. Follow the directions on the survey when you are addressing a particular dimension of your life.

Survey: Hallmarks of an Effective Follower

- Give yourself a follower "strength test" score of 1 low to 10 high for each hallmark as it relates to the particular dimension of your life you are assessing.

- List some supporting evidence for the score you've given to each hallmark in the space below.

- Validate the accuracy of your perceptions by sharing them with an accountability partner and getting his or her feedback.

- Review your results and set some personal growth goals for becoming a more effective follower in this dimension of your life.

My intent is to be a high-integrity follower when appropriate. The relative strength I believe I possess, related to each hallmark at this time, is listed below with supporting evidence.

1. Manage myself well

2. Am committed to the organization I'm engaged in

3. Respect legitimate authority

4. Seek specific directions

5. Accept significant assignments

6. Diligently develop my competencies and credibility

7. Focus my efforts for maximum impact

8. Value honest appraisals and feedback

9. Exhibit exemplary integrity and honesty

10. Am courageous and confront wrong behavior

11. Have published and distributed my Followers Credo

You know that personal freedom does not limit your ethical responsibility; that powerful ethical standards for conduct do not protect you from temptation toward moral compromise; that innocent vulnerability can lead to actions and accusations of ethical abandonment; that personal ethical integrity does not insure you against wrongful judgments.

Unlike ineffective followers, your conduct is legal and ethical; and you never settle for one or the other for your own convenience or gain. You also know that consistently living your life based on high ethical standards for conduct will enable you to enjoy ultimate exoneration if falsely accused.

10. *You are courageous and confront wrong behavior.* You are a person who will not let evil succeed by doing nothing. You are skillful at the art of confrontation and are determined to use it so that right action prevails and wrong action fails. As you confront wrong actions, you respond to fact, not fantasy, and go beyond personal fears. You take responsibility for ensuring justice and make sure the issue passes the "reasonable person" test as you tell the truth with a spirit of mercy.

Unlike ineffective followers, you don't worry about confrontation being comfortable or risky. You don't avoid it, even if the cost is high, because you know that right action ultimately leads to right results; wrong action ultimately leads to wrong results. It is as sure as the law of gravity!

Think about what you already know regarding the life of Jesus as a follower and leader. Identify places in the Bible that illustrate Him exhibiting each of these ten hallmarks. Examine the lives of the disciples and the lives of other leaders throughout the Bible to see if you can find examples of these hallmarks in action. Also, search for examples of people in the Bible who failed to express one or more of the hallmarks and the consequences that resulted from not being an effective follower. You'll find fascinating examples of right action and wrong action as it pertains to the skill of following.

My Credo as an Effective Follower

I am committed to serving others as an effective follower when the situation calls for it within all organizations in which I serve. I appreciate being associated with colleagues who are competent at both leading and following and respect the value of both. I will not use my legitimate authority to avoid following others when it is right to do so.

As an effective follower my intent is to serve within, achieving the vision, values, mission, and goals of our organization by

- managing myself well before attempting to lead others,
- demonstrating commitment to the organization I'm engaged in,
- respecting legitimate authority,
- seeking specific directions,
- accepting significant assignments,
- diligently developing my competencies and credibility,
- focusing my efforts for maximum impact,
- valuing honest appraisals and feedback,
- exhibiting exemplary integrity and honesty,
- being courageous and confronting wrong behavior.

TIME OUT!

Write your own Follower's Credo.

Followers Credo

To help you grow in your ability to follow others appropriately, you can develop your own credo as a follower. Sharing it with family and colleagues at work sends a loud message about the importance you attach to being a good follower and positions you to engage others in holding you accountable for expressing the hallmarks of a good follower. It also positions you to encourage them to become better followers for everyone's benefit. Here is an example of a follower's credo.

I urge you to risk, reach out, and share your credo as a follower with your family first. When you are comfortable with the role of being an effective follower at home, it is time to take your credo to your work place. At home or work, it makes a great statement and is a strong visual reinforcement if you type your credo, frame it, and hang it on a wall. This strategy will empower others to strengthen their follower skills and it will empower you!

TAKE A "WHEEL TRUING" TIME OUT!

Work on Any One of the Spokes You Haven't Yet "Trued"

Please turn to appendix A for guide questions.

7

LEADERSHIP SKILLS

I treasure a copy of a large ad placed by the United Technologies Corporation in 1984. The title is, "LET'S GET RID OF MAN-AGEMENT." The ad says,

> People don't want to be managed. They want to be led. Whoever heard of a world manager? World leader, yes. Educational leader. Political leader. Religious leader. Labor leader. Business leader. Scout leader. Community leader. They lead. They don't manage. The carrot always wins over the stick. Ask your horse. You can lead your horse to water but you can't manage him to drink. If you want to manage somebody, manage yourself. Do that well and you'll be ready to stop managing. And start leading.

Many legitimate leaders who head up families, businesses, churches, and schools are behaving as if they still haven't learned their lessons from their "horse" experiences. I often wonder, *Do they really care if their "horses" drink the water and remain healthy, vital, and productive?*

Who are the "horses" you're responsible to lead? Your spouse? Your children? Other relatives? Your staff members and colleagues at work? Your boss? People at church?

THE DIFFERENCE BETWEEN LEADERSHIP AND MANAGEMENT

Leadership is a people process. It calls for the application of knowledge, skills, and attitudes that allow each of us to successfully influence and inspire others toward doing the right things. Leadership deals with effectiveness. On the other hand, management is a coordinating process we carry out to make sure the work functions and tasks get done well and in a timely way. The management function also requires keeping a thrifty eye on the use of time, materials, energy, and money by scheduling, allotting, budgeting, and other *manageable* things. The function of management focuses on efficiency—doing things right. I believe it is imperative that all stakeholders in our homes, churches, schools, and workplaces carry out both functions to the best of their abilities.

The chart below gives you a quick guide for clarifying which role you are in to achieve a particular purpose and result. It will also help you determine if your focus and actions are congruent with your intended role as either a leader or manager.

Knowing the Difference	Leadership	Management
Focus	People	Resources
Actions	Influence and Inspire	Coordinate
Result	Effectiveness	Efficiency

WHO SHOULD BE A LEADER?

Doesn't it make sense that everyone should be encouraged to develop and apply the skills of leadership? Young children and adults in homes and managers and workers in organizations can be taught how to lead effectively when they have a clear vision, established values, a mission, and goals.

The most common obstacle to leadership is lack of a clear vision, operating values, mission, and goals. On the other hand, proactive leaders and the organizations they serve have identified and communicated values that are based on a firm standard. These values give people the foundation for developing system-wide accountability in terms of ethical conduct, quality performance, and service.

I believe it is wise to base personal and organizational values on those found in the Bible—the only source of irrefutable truth and logical personal practices. God instructs us to be servant-leaders and to love people. In a functional sense He is speaking to all of us, not just those who are the designated leaders of the home, school, church, or organization!

HALLMARKS OF A SERVICE-ORIENTED LEADER

Many excellent authors have written books about what it takes to be a successful leader. Stephen Covey, in his best-seller, *The Seven Habits of Highly Effective People*, addressed a number of solid leadership principles as he elaborated on each habit. Burt Nanus, in his book, *Visionary Leadership*, did a wonderful job of describing what effective leaders do. Merrill Oster, in his book, *Vision-Driven Leadership*, shared some great stories and principles.

I won't share much about the "stuff" of leadership, which has been written about so well by others. What I want to do is help you focus on leadership characteristics that God has established that work in all places and in all situations.

Over the years I've often asked workshop participants to do this exercise: "Think of the most outstanding leader you've ever followed. List the characteristics and attributes that motivated you to follow him or her and eagerly collaborate with them as you achieved the work of your organization."

I kept the information I gathered from workshops for years! I knew there were common threads in the boxes of cards and charts I had saved, and I wanted to get it all boiled down to a usable list. I tried and tried over time but never pulled together a single list that captured the most frequently identified attributes of outstanding leaders.

One day I was reading 1 Corinthians 13 where Paul spelled out the attributes of a loving servant. As I stopped to read it again, I realized that these verses captured the essentials of what people had been telling me were the most important characteristics of the kind of leader they wanted to follow.

I converted the list of characteristics to positive terms and have used them ever since as a starting point in many of my workshops. They are God's proven principles for relating to people *and they work every time.* They have also proven to be very profitable characteristics that support long-term careers and healthy profit margins for organizations.

Service-oriented leaders who possess these characteristics draw loyal and productive followers like magnets. These leaders are successful at home and in the workplace. Such leaders provide the kind of interpersonal relationship support that motivates the people they lead to consistently exhibit their best. People enjoy helping such leaders accomplish the work. What characteristics do these leaders display?

Patience. You are patient with people. Your patience is heartfelt and translates to overt actions and calmness as you deal with people in situations that test your patience. You recognize their strengths and short suits and accept them where they are. You also help them to set goals to become more than they presently are in terms of character, competence, and commitment.

Kindness. Even when people are unkind to you, you are courteous and respond to them with a kind heart, even in the heat of conflict.

Gratitude. People respond well to your appreciative remarks, notes, and gestures. You are aware of what others are doing and let them know specifically what they have done to help the quality of the work, and you describe their contribution and personal value to the team. You show gratitude regularly and in a timely way that reinforces their desire to keep doing the things that please you.

Graciousness. You are compassionate and let people know that you enjoy them and enjoy being in their presence. You quickly give credit to others when it is due. You help others as quickly as possible when they need it and you do it in a supportive, coaching kind of way.

Humility. Others never get a "better than you" message from your words, tone of voice, or actions. You genuinely view others as equal partners with different responsibilities, talents, and gifts as together you make the enterprise successful.

Politeness. Courteous remarks and good manners are your hall-mark and people feel good being around you. You remain civil even when attacked by others and you show class and refinement wherever you are.

Generosity. Your eyes and ears are wide open as you seek opportunities to give in a heartfelt way to others. You are a giver rather than a taker.

Calm Understanding. When the arrows of battle fly your way, you assess the situation and the mindset and emotions of the people around you. You contribute to bringing order to chaos.

Justice. When injustice occurs within your sphere of leadership, you confront it and help to make things right as soon as possible.

Truth. To the best of your ability you speak only the truth. You avoid silence or withholding the truth when questioned by others or when they will benefit from hearing it even if they don't ask. You speak in clear language that has little chance of being misunderstood. Your facial expressions, body language and vocal tone are congruent with the words of truth you speak.

Forgiveness. If others blow it, you help them assess what went wrong and help them plan preventive steps to ensure it doesn't happen again. You encourage people to view mistakes as learning opportunities and to let their past errors go, both emotionally and mentally.

Protection. When things seem out of balance and unfair, you help others maintain their rights and protect their legitimate interests. You lead the charge in making sure others are not taken advantage of.

Trust. As people drop the ball and fail to keep their promises, you assertively confront them about the situation without demeaning or soft-soaping the situation. You help them to understand their attitudes, motivations, and commitment, and you encourage them to be promise-keepers. You also help and encourage them to be more responsible in making promises by being sure their *yes* is a yes and their *no* is a no.

Hope. You keep a positive attitude and have abundant belief that things can and will improve, even when they are going poorly, seem to be falling apart, and interpersonal conflict is on the rise.

Expectation. Mediocrity, a halfhearted attitude, and a half-done job are not acceptable to you. You exemplify the work ethic and expect others to expect the best from you. You also make it clear that you expect their best in return. You don't give up on people and settle for less.

Loyalty. Face-to-face straight talk is what you give people. You never talk about others behind their backs or repeat gossip. In fact, you do all you can to stop gossip by facilitating face-to-face dialogue and problem-solving of concerns and gripes that come your way. You also make clear to people the boundaries and conditions you have for being loyal to them.

Perseverance. "Try and try again" is your pattern when you're attempting to achieve a worthwhile result. You don't give up easily and you keep going—whether you're trying to improve difficult relationships with others or completing tough tasks and projects.

Good Will. Your heart contains no ill will toward anyone. You do, however, have preferences for people you socialize with, political views you hold, and the values you live. Still, you consistently possess and express an attitude of goodwill toward all people.

HOW TO FOCUS ON BEING A PROACTIVE, SERVICE-ORIENTED LEADER

I've named my consulting practice ProActive Leadership Consulting & Training. I split the word *proactive* into two parts to put an emphasis on the *Pro* and *Active* as two separate components of leadership. The *Pro* is a reminder of the professional knowledge, skills, and attitudes needed to influence and inspire others. The *Active* is a reminder that the knowledge, skills, and attitudes we possess must be regularly and competently applied to be useful to us and to benefit others.

A primary step I took toward becoming a more proactive, servant-oriented leader was to carefully take stock of Jesus Christ in action and ask myself, "What would Jesus do?" when I was trying to influence and inspire other people to think, say, and do the right thing. I read the Bible carefully, seeking to understand what it says about relating to people, serving them, and following His example. Understanding and loving people is what value-driven, proactive leadership is all about. Christ is the greatest leader of all time! Use Him as your model.

What characteristics did Jesus model as a leader? His words and actions consistently reinforced each other. Throughout His ministry, Jesus was:

- A *visionary* who constantly focused on the future. (Matt. 5:1–12)
- A *listener* who had the desire and ability to listen to others. (Luke 10:38–42)
- *Responsive* to what he heard by connecting to people. (Mark 5:21–43)
- *Authentic* and did not try to impress people. (Mark 14:34)
- *Compassionate* by entering into places of pain and crying out and mourning with those in misery. (Matt. 9:36)
- *Forgiving* by freely taking away people's burdens and freeing them from past mistakes. (John 8:1–11)
- *Straightforward* by being sincere and candid. (Mark 2:23–28)
- *Generative* by being other-centered, building relationships, and producing disciples to carry on His vision and mission. (John 15:5–8)
- *Inclusive* by not being prejudiced or condemning and by being open and loving toward all people. (Matt. 28:19)
- *Empowering* by giving others the responsibility and power to carry out the mission. (John 15–16)
- *Full of integrity* by being committed to doing the right thing regardless of consequences, and by helping others define and reflect on the values that drive their decisions and behaviors. (John 19:11).

Being a loving, servant-oriented, value-driven leader is not natural for us, given our basic nature. Being this kind of leader calls for taking the focus off of the "me" and putting the focus on serving "others." However, with the Holy Spirit's help and a strong personal intent, you and I can be transformed into this kind of Christlike leader. We can strengthen our loving responses so that we express the excellence of love Paul described so well in 1 Corinthians 13:4–7, "Love is patient, love is kind. It does not envy, it does not boast, it is not proud. It is not rude, it is not self-seeking, it is

---

TIME OUT! *Write in your notebook . . .*
10 minutes on each characteristic.

Write on what each leadership characteristic means to you. Specifically ask yourself, "How can I best express each characteristic in the different areas of my life as I inspire and influence others to do the right things? Keeping the Lord as your leadership model, reflect daily on a different characteristic and how it applies to one of the areas of your life. Do this and you will experience significant growth as a leader!

---

not easily angered, it keeps no record of wrongs. Love does not delight in evil but rejoices with the truth. It always protects, always trusts, always hopes, always perseveres."

When I first developed the Hallmarks of a ProActive Leader Survey, I was having a tough time consistently practicing several of the hallmarks of love. As I read 1 Corinthians 13 and Galatians 5:22–25, I recognized clearly that I was not the loving, proactive, service-oriented leader at home or work that I thought I was.

I decided that I must, out of my love for the Lord, more diligently go about the work of accommodating His character and nature into my own. I knew that the message and the messenger had to be congruent if I had any chance of inspiring and influencing others to shift away from conditional integrity toward God's operational paradigm of intentional integrity.

As I started this journey, I was particularly challenged by the first hallmark of love Paul talked about—patience. I started filling out my new survey at the end of each week during my regular morning Bible study and prayer time. This gave me a fix on how I was doing, particularly with the issues of patience and calm understanding, two of my spiritual growth goals. Taking the time to actually list the testy situations where God's grace helped me express loving patience and calm understanding, as well as the situations where I had expressed impatience, helped me to pinpoint areas for further growth. Barbara also filled out the survey from time to time, giving me valuable feedback.

Try using the feedback survey once a week for three months to see how well you're manifesting the hallmarks of a loving, service-oriented leader.

Ask others you trust to fill out the survey for you as well. The survey items are constructed so that you can easily translate one or more of them into spiritual growth goal statements. As you get feedback and set goals, you will increase your competency in expressing these hallmarks. You will also be able to more quickly and easily influence and inspire others to do the right things because you're modeling love.

Survey: Hallmarks of a ProActive, Service-Oriented Leader

To help you reflect on your interpersonal effectiveness as a ProActive Leader:

- Mark the degree (1 low - 10 high) to which you see yourself manifesting each of the hallmarks below.

- Write specific examples of what you do to manifest each hallmark.

- Write out your personal growth goals for enhancing one or more of these hallmarks and work toward their achievement.

- Share your goals with an "accountability partner" or members of your management team.

- Monitor your progress and celebrate successes!

- To what degree do you

   1. ☐ demonstrate *patience* in doing work and interacting with people?

   2. ☐ express *kindness* toward all persons?

   3. ☐ show *gratitude* at home and work?

   4. ☐ demonstrate *graciousness* in dealing with people?

5. ☐ serve family, colleagues, and others with a *humble* spirit?

6. ☐ demonstrate *politeness* in word and deed?

7. ☐ demonstrate that *giving* and *serving* are deeply held values?

8. ☐ express *calm understanding* in dealing with conflict?

9. ☐ show delight in promoting *justice?*

10. ☐ bring the *truth* to bear in all situations?

11. ☐ reach out to *forgive* mistakes and faults?

12. ☐ work diligently to *protect people's interests?*

13. ☐ show *trust* in others?

14. ☐ demonstrate *hope* in difficult situations?

15. ☐ show that you *expect* the *best* from others?

16. ☐ demonstrate *loyalty* to others?

17. ☐ show *perseverance* in achieving results?

18. ☐ manifest *good will* in word and deed?[9]

TIME OUT! *Reflect on: What? So What? and Now What?*

Key Reflections

1. What are the attributes of an effective leader you think are worth emulating?
2. What benefits will accrue to you and others as you develop and nurture these?
3. What steps are you going to take to strengthen your impact as a leader?

DEVELOPING AND LEVERAGING YOUR LEADERSHIP CREDO

As a leader it is important to recognize there are two sides to the "golden coin" of leadership: the substantive *and* the symbolic. Both are important for long-term success. You may deeply value worship and spend time at 5 A.M. praying, studying the Bible, and thinking about how you're going to apply what you've learned. This is a *substantive* aspect of personal worship as a leader in your home. If no one in your family sees you worshiping, is involved with you in worship, or hears you talk about the importance of worshiping and personally obeying God's Word, you have failed to communicate the *symbolic* messages that let them know that worshiping, obedience, and leading your family in worship are important to you. Proactive leaders first focus on the substantive aspects of their leadership, then back up the substance with solid symbolic messages that make clear their leadership values.

A powerful way to send a message about your leadership values is to develop a personal leadership credo, publish it and share it with those in your spheres of leadership. Display it prominently. Sincerely encourage everyone to help you be accountable for living the values you express in your credo. You can also miniaturize it and keep it in your purse or wallet. If you are a business executive you can develop a Corporate Credo which can be published in newsletters and annual reports or displayed at the entrance to your company's building.

Be clear, however, that the substantive aspects of your credo come first in importance. The symbolic act of displaying a credo is shallow if the substance is not behind it. There is nothing more impotent than a credo which lies dormant in your brain and has no positive and worthwhile influence on your behavior, your life and the lives of others. Ensure, to the best of your ability, that all of your convictions and operating values are translated into practice and that all of your practice is based on your convictions and operating values.

My Credo as a Husband and Father

My commitment to God, myself, my wife, and family members is that I will hold myself accountable and encourage my family members to hold me accountable for thinking, saying, and doing the right things, according to God's will and commands, by

- Praying and reading God's Word daily to gain the wisdom to help me better *know, love, and glorify* God; become more Christlike in thought and action; understand His plan; and participate with Him and others in His plan.

- *Loving* my wife, children, and grandchildren as Christ wants me to love them.

- Demonstrating *good stewardship* of the time, talent, and treasure God has given me by strategically using the time, spiritual gifts (faith, leadership, administration, teaching, wisdom, and discernment), and financial resources God has given to me in the most beneficial ways possible.

- Showing *godly leadership* in my family and never using my legitimate authority alone to attempt to gain respect and get results.

- Demonstrating that *giving and serving* are deeply held values.

- Serving my family with a *humble* spirit.

- Demonstrating *hope* in difficult situations by reaching out to family members with my head, heart, and hands to help them address their difficulties and opportunities.

- Demonstrating *loyalty* to each family member.

- Expressing *kindness* toward each family member.

- Demonstrating *graciousness* in dealing with each family member.

- Being a *self-starter* by creating plans and engaging other family members in the creation of plans with a worthwhile vision driven by godly values.

- *Diligently* achieving worthwhile results and encouraging each family member to do the same.

- Demonstrating *patience* in all encounters with family members and the work I do at home.
- Maintaining a *sense of humor* and laughing at myself.
- Showing *gratitude* to each family member.
- Demonstrating *politeness* in word and deed.
- Expressing *calm understanding* when dealing with difficult situations.
- *Forgiving* mistakes and faults in myself and my family members.
- Manifesting *good will* in word and deed.

My Credo as a ProActive Leader

I am committed to serving others and to facilitating the intentional integrity paradigm in all organizations I serve. I want to be associated with proactive colleagues of high character and competence and earn my recognition as a leader of integrity and competence. I will not use my legitimate authority to attempt to gain respect and get results in my sphere of leadership. As a Pro Active Leader,

- I focus on *serving* others. To effectively inspire and influence others to think, say, and do the right things, I know that I must first be a servant to them; model value-driven, service-oriented leadership practices; and make every effort to *think, say, and do the right things*.
- I desire to see things through the eyes of others and help them think, say, and do the right things so that they achieve their worthwhile goals more quickly and easily.
- I challenge others with, "Let's go!" lead the way, and then help them get out in front. I assume that others are working in collaboration and cooperation with me, not for me. I consider them partners in the work and see to it that they share in the rewards. I promote team spirit.

- I nurture leadership in others. I am a people-builder. I help those I work with to grow in character, competence, and commitment. I realize that the more excellent people an organization has, the stronger it will be in terms of *credibility, longevity, and financial stability.*

- I lift people up by reaching out to them with my mind, my hands, and my heart to help them climb tall mountains and hike out of troublesome valleys. After I have looked at the facts with my head I let my heart take a look. Even when I am in charge, I am also a friend.

- I have a deep faith in the potential in people. I believe in them, trust them, and help them draw out the best in themselves. I find that they usually rise to my high expectations regarding *character, competence, and commitment.*

- I am a self-starter. I create plans and engage others in the creation of plans with a vision, operating values, missions, and goals. I work diligently and expect others to do the same. I am both a person of thought and action—both a visionary and a doer.

- I have a sense of humor. I can laugh at myself. I have a humble spirit.

- I can be led by others. I am not interested in having my own way but in finding the right way to achieve the vision, mission, and goals in line with our values. I am open to receiving affirmative and corrective feedback that will help me maintain and enhance my own performance as it is manifested through *my own character, competence, and commitment.*

- I keep my eyes on a *noble* vision and make every effort to bring it to realization with *worthwhile* values, missions, and goals. I strive to ensure that my performance behavior and those of others I work with achieve the right results. I hold myself and my colleagues accountable for thinking, saying, and doing the right things so we all contribute to strengthening the integrity of our organization's people, processes, policies, and products, as well as the organization's long-term financial strength.

TIME OUT!
Write a draft of your Leadership Credo.

After you've completed your first draft, share it with a few people you trust. Get feedback about it. Ask them open-ended questions such as, "Where is it clear and unclear?" "Where does it come across as sincere or insincere?" "What parts of it establish clear expectations?"

When your credo is ready, share it with the people around you and enjoy the many benefits from taking an open stand as a leader!

TAKE A "WHEEL TRUING" TIME OUT!

Work on any one of the spokes you haven't yet "trued."

Please Turn to appendix A for guide questions.

8

ADAPTIVE SKILLS

As a relatively new manager, I was walking down the office hallway one day and greeted Sue, one of my team members. I noted the frown on her face and her tight lips as she gave me an unmotivated "Hi." I could tell she was in a hurry and let it go at the time, but I knew something was wrong.

Later that day, I saw Sue again and asked her if she had a few minutes for us to talk. Over a cup of coffee I asked her if anything was wrong. She stiffened as I described our encounter in the hallway that morning and her eyes began to tear. I was embarrassed.

Finally I said, "Sue, have I done something to offend you?" She answered no, with the same frown on her face and the tight lips. "Something is going on," I said. "What is it?"

With that, she gave me both barrels. She told me it wasn't what I had done, it was what I hadn't done! She told me I was one of the most closed persons to feedback she had ever known and that I didn't listen to her. She told me how she had tried to give me feedback at a meeting over three weeks before about her concerns over a project our team was working on. She described in detail how I, as her manager, had become defensive, brushed off her concerns as insignificant and rolled on. To say the least, I was taken aback. I told her so. I also told her that regardless of how upset I was to hear this, I very much appreciated her taking the risk to be honest and direct with me. I also told her I needed to take some time to look hard at my behavior if it was affecting a top team player like herself so negatively.

I learned a lot as I explored the issue with my other colleagues. They validated that I was lousy at soliciting, listening to, and receiving feedback. This experience taught me the importance of "adaptive skills." I'm forever grateful to Sue, because my efforts to develop and hone these skills have paid off.

THREE TYPES OF SKILLS

Each of us possesses to one degree or another three types of skills: Technical Skills, Basic Skills, and Adaptive Skills.[10]

Your *Technical Skills Bank* is made up of the competencies that enable you to do a particular type of work quickly and correctly. Computer programming, eye surgery, construction, French cooking, hair cutting, teaching math are all banks of technical skills needed to accomplish particular types of work at home or in the work place.

Your *Basic Skills Bank* contains skills that are transferable to many work settings and are used along with technical skills in order to get work accomplished. Planning, writing, speaking, organizing, and problem solving are examples of these skills.

Your *Adaptive Skills Bank* contains the competencies you began to develop when you were very young and are now played out as you interact with your environment—home, school, or work.

This Skill Bank is most often neglected. How you went about adapting to your environment as a child has a lot to do with how you are able to get along with authority figures now. Your adaptability also impacts the accuracy of your self-concept, how you handle comments and critiques from others, and how open you are to expressing your feelings appropriately and forthrightly.

THIRTEEN KEY ADAPTIVE SKILLS

When you're working with people, a shortage of adaptive skills will cause you problems because a shortage of these skills thwarts your interpersonal abilities to lead others and restricts your personal growth potential. If you have a shortage of adaptive skills you will have difficulty working through and resolving interpersonal conflicts even if your technical and basic skills are outstanding. This is why it's important to strengthen your adaptive skills and make them an integral part of your Personal Integrity Management process.

SKILL 1: PARTICIPATING IN LEARNING EXPERIENCES

Since the success of much your work is based on more than your technical and basic competencies, you can't just "measure up" in these areas and have no further problems. You interface with other people—spouse, children, colleagues, bosses and customers—and are in interdependent relationships with them. Working and learning in concert with others is unavoidable unless you are a hermit or do research in an isolated rain forest.

If you have a hard time involving yourself in new learning experiences, you may fear that you are inadequate or believe that if people discover the "real you" they will see through your façade and will not like or respect what they see. Even if you are like many people and are uneasy about taking risks and learning with others, it is essential to confront your uneasiness and grow in your ability to deal with it. Articulating your uneasiness and sharing it with others is a positive first step forward!

SKILL 2: RESPONDING TO LEGITIMATE AUTHORITY

Responding appropriately to your boss or others who have legitimate authority is one of the most important sets of adaptive skills you can possess. When you relate to someone who has legitimate authority over you, you bring your personal views, understanding, biases, and hang-ups regarding authority into the relationship. You may interact with them from a stance of dependence, independence, interdependence, or counter-dependence (when your boss is highly dependent upon you), depending on the situation.

One way to identify how you relate to authority figures is through "story telling." Have a trusted friend let you tell them your favorite and not-so-favorite boss stories, spouse stories, and teacher stories. Tape-record your session and play it back. Listen to the tape carefully with your friend, and both of you make notes as to what your expressed attitudes, emotional tones, and values seemed to be regarding your relationship to the authority in each story. Share your insights with your friend and have him or her share with you. This process will give you solid insights into how you relate to authority and will help you improve how you interact with authority in future situations.

SKILL 3: EXERCISING YOUR OWN AUTHORITY

You possess your own areas of expertise and abilities that your boss or other employees may not possess. You *are* an authority!

I once had a secretary who had a hard time exercising her own authority. I had difficulty convincing her it was okay to make mistakes and that we would both learn from those we made, singly or together. I told her over and over again that I trusted her judgment to make certain decisions on my behalf when I wasn't in the office.

Do you claim, maintain, and effectively use your personal authority to influence your boss and other people to do the right things, to get work done in better, faster, and easier ways? Do you do this even when you don't have the legitimate authority of a position? If your knowledge is sound and your skills are strong, it is important that you place yourself in a position of temporary authority and leadership to help your boss and colleagues do the right things in the right way to achieve the worthwhile vision, mission, and goals of the organization employing you.

The direct approach works well for me. I analyze the situation out loud and spell out for the person or persons involved what I see as needed in terms of action steps and leadership. I review for them how my character traits, competencies, and commitment to guiding the situation to a worthwhile conclusion can help everyone if they are willing to give me permission (authority) to lead for the moment and follow me until we achieve the results we all want.

SKILL 4: COMMUNICATING EMOTIONS/FEELINGS

As a highly adaptive person you'll want to be tuned to your emotional state as your emotions and feelings surface. Being in tune with your emotions and feelings enables you to do what's appropriate with them in a given situation. I define emotions as those "hair-raising" emotive expressions such as fear, anger, hurt, blame, and frustration. It is helpful to distinguish emotions that tend to get us into trouble as we relate to other people from feelings (such as love, kindness, gratitude, and warmth), which usually help us build closeness, understanding, and good relationships. Remember, however, *there are no right or wrong feelings or emotions.* They are present when they are present! If you're like me, your emotions and feelings often seem to have a will of their own and surface or dissipate without you having much control over them.

The goal is to recognize your emotions and feelings and use them creatively and constructively in your relationships with other people. Our emotions and feelings are protective and expressive responses triggered in our subconscious minds. They are designed to serve us when experiencing stress or pleasure.

The problem with communicating emotions and feelings to others is that the only clues others have about our emotions and feelings are what show on the outside. Things like vocal tone, eye expression, facial expression, body proximity, and other nonverbal behaviors communicate more about our emotions and feelings than do our words. How often do you verbally express the content of your feelings and emotions? Occasionally? Frequently? Never? Are there certain emotional states you will allow others to see and others you hide, depending on the person you're relating with? High-integrity people act in ways that match their emotions. They let others know, in appropriate ways, when they are angry, sad, afraid, or glad. I'll describe some specific interpersonal feedback principles in chapter 10 on Communication Skills.

SKILL 5: RECEIVING FEEDBACK

When you are committed to the integrity of what you think, say, and do you will view corrective feedback from others as pure gold and seek it. Think about it. All performance champions in any field depend on feedback. Most are tenacious about asking others for it.

This includes football players, pilots, attorneys, doctors, teachers, spouses, and children. Like it or not, we all receive different forms of corrective and affirmative feedback from other people at home and work most every day of our lives.

How effectively you receive feedback is a critical adaptive skill. Your success in employing this skill is most likely related to your experiences of feedback as a young child. If your experiences were painful or humiliating, you may have a tendency to resent and resist feedback from others, particularly adults with legitimate authority.

If your parents, siblings, teachers, and best friends gave you corrective and affirmative feedback in ways that caused you to experience a great deal of acceptance, you're probably less tense and defensive about feedback from others at home and at work.

As a person of intentional integrity you'll want to hone your ability to be open to receiving feedback by

1. being quick to sense your feelings of defensiveness as they surface;

2. holding yourself back from arguing with the person giving you the feedback;

3. listening attentively to the person;

4. kindly concluding the feedback episode by saying to them something like, "Thanks for your feedback. I know it was as hard for you to share as it is for me to receive. I really appreciate your forthrightness, and I'll seriously think about what you've just told me."

Remember, your goal *is not* to focus on receiving corrective feedback nondefensively. To maintain your adaptive edge, develop your skill in *being aware* of your defensiveness. Be able to describe it to yourself and the other person in a way that you can get enough distance from it to be receptive to feedback. Two questions to jolt you out of your defensiveness and get you into the other person's frame of reference are, "What kind of risk is this person taking when they take the time and initiative to give me corrective feedback?" and "Would I do the same for them?"

SKILL 6: GIVING FEEDBACK

As I've developed a greater value and appreciation for receiving feedback, I see it as an incredible opportunity to learn and grow. It's also grown me in my ability to give feedback in more direct and timely ways and with more genuine care and compassion.

As you relate to others, you may find it difficult to give each other helpful information because you do not know how to give accurate, objective feedback. You may not want to say anything unless it is good. You may be trying to "protect them." If this is so, you'll not share with others what they most desperately need to hear!

Or you may be at the other extreme. Some people are able to toss out criticism like a terrorist's bomb and then disappear safely out of reach of the explosion. If you fit either extreme you need to work on strengthening your feedback skills. As you do, you'll become more adaptive and a person of greater integrity.

The feedback you receive from other people and that you give to other people is usually loaded with the inferences, judgments, and projections of the person giving it. You are most likely giving feedback filtered by your own issues, values, and feelings about the other person! Again, I'll be sharing more about principles for giving and receiving feedback in chapter 10 on communication skills.

SKILL 7: FACILITATING SELF-CORRECTION

This adaptive skill has to do with what you do with the feedback you receive from others. You may be a person who deflects it, denies it, explains it away, or in some other way tries to keep from taking personal responsibility and responding to it. As a high-integrity, adaptive person you'll be able to stay open to the feedback, even when you feel defensive. You'll be able to share with other people that you are feeling defensive and encourage them to continue the process until you understand what they are trying to tell you. You can then demonstrate your appreciation to them for taking the risk to help you grow.

The degree to which you feel defensive often means that the feedback someone is trying to give you is getting close to something very important for you to learn. Learning about yourself at these pinch points will more often than not help you grow and go to higher levels of personal integrity and help you gain and maintain better balance in your life.

As you become highly skilled in learning about yourself and making corrections, you'll find yourself asking for feedback. It is a way to learn from your mistakes and make significant progress toward thinking, saying, and doing the right things.

SKILL 8: MAINTAINING AN ACCURATE SELF-CONCEPT

Years ago I worked with a guy named Tom. Tom also had fragile and explosive sides to his nature. He was easily hurt and easily angered. He saw neither propensity. He saw himself as expressing honesty and forthrightness when his emotions blew into hurt, blame, or anger. No one would tell him the truth about himself, including me, because we all feared being drug into his pity parties or bearing the brunt of his blame or anger. As a result of not being able to solicit and receive feedback about his behavior, Tom gave the rest of us an illegitimate excuse for not giving him feedback in a caring and forthright way. This was wrong for Tom and wrong for us.

The terms *self-esteem*, *self-image*, and *self-concept* have been used interchangeably by different authors. Therefore I've developed the following definitions to facilitate communication between myself and my clients.

- *Self-concept* is the result of how you conceptualize your actual self, the "real you," No more or no less than you are. Your concept of yourself as others see you and as God sees you needs to be accurate and based on reality. However, it can also be distorted, inaccurate, and based on illusions or delusions.

- *Self-image* is your picture of the ideal likeness or representation you want to become. It is what you want your physical body, character, and competence to look like—a sort of preferred state of being and functioning.

- *Self-esteem* is how good you feel about the degree of congruence between your self-concept and your self-image. It is how much you respect, honor, admire, and regard who you are and how you behave.

The skill of gaining and maintaining an accurate self-concept is critical to maintaining your personal integrity and to supporting your efforts to align what you see (concept) with what you want to be (image) so that you'll feel right (esteem) about yourself as you live life and relate to others.

Self-concept, as I'm using the term, is how you see yourself, accurately or inaccurately. Your looks, your height, your weight, your character, your competence, your commitment are just a few of the dimensions of the "real you."

The concept of humility is related to an accurate self-concept. One of the features of love that Paul talked about in 1 Corinthians 13 is humility. Possessing this quality in today's world may cause you to be viewed as "wimpy" or a "push-over" and certainly not assertive. However, humility, as the Bible describes it, doesn't mean putting yourself down. It means to possess an accurate self-concept, which includes knowing who you are in God's eyes, that He created you, and that Jesus Christ came to earth and purchased you for a price! It means recognizing the truth about your human strengths and short suits, your character traits, your competencies, your physical and mental abilities, and your talents. It means seeing yourself no better or worse than you really are.

Humility will allow you to accept yourself as you presently are, help you see yourself more accurately and know what you are capable and not capable of doing. It will help you determine what you need to do to become a high integrity person.

SKILL 9: ADAPTING TO REALITY

As you go through the process of gaining a more accurate self-concept and aligning it with your self-image, you'll most likely experience one or more of three basic scenarios.

1. Your esteem will be high with moments of feeling down.
2. You'll feel down most of the time with wonderful moments of feeling up or acceptable.
3. You'll be on a stable course where the peaks and valleys you experience are not very often and are very small.

If you experience scenario one, you may at times think that you're "big time." During these ups you may actually be out of touch with some of your most important short suits—those that may be keeping you from growing and going to your highest level of functioning and balance.

The second scenario may cause you to be frozen by feelings of inadequacy, even though you may actually be very capable and proficient but don't recognize or accept it.

When you find yourself in the third scenario, check to make sure you are not out of touch with your up and down emotions by having learned to protect yourself by denying changes in your emotional state.

The key to having the ability to adapt to reality is to ensure that you don't assume that any of your emotional extremes are rational or are an accurate representation of reality. You need to be aware of them, experience them, but not base your judgments about yourself on them. Your actual competence and character is not connected to your feelings about your competence and character.

It is important to develop the ability to step back from your emotions while watching yourself experience them. At the same time you need to accurately assess the real value of whatever you're contributing to any situation.

When you experience large peaks and valleys in your emotions related to your esteem, they may not be related to your actual competence or character. However, it would be wise to examine those feelings. Such an examination can reveal elements in the situation that triggered your feelings of inadequacy in the first place.

Later, in chapter 9 on Peacemaker Skills, we'll discuss tools that will help you identify any wrong thinking that may be creating distortions in the accuracy of the concept you have of yourself. Also the distortions in the reality of the concepts you have of others with whom you experience recurring interpersonal conflicts.

SKILL 10: AWARENESS OF IMPACT ON OTHERS

This adaptive skill is difficult for most of us to develop fully. To this day I tend to miss the nonverbal language coming from people unless it roars out like the Columbia River going to the ocean.

During my first year as a new principal of an inner-city elementary school in Los Angeles, I was blessed with a great staff, one of them being Margaret Smart. Miss Smart was a sixty-year-old kindergarten teacher par excellence!

I had a "thing" about educators receiving gifts and gratuities. One day, I found a box and card on my desk on my birthday. It was from Margaret. It was a tie and $10 with a note on the card asking me to buy the style of shirt I would like best to match the tie. I felt embarrassed and a little upset. I immediately set out down the hall to find Margaret during the first recess.

As I approached her she had a big smile on her face. I told her how much I appreciated her nice gesture, but that I could not accept gifts from faculty members.

She burst out in tears and with great sobs told me that I didn't like her. I had no idea what to do. Finally in the middle of her sobs, I pulled myself together and just put my arm gently around her shoulder and said a quiet and humble "Thanks." I also told her again how much I liked her and appreciated her great work with our kids.

What I had completely overlooked about Margaret was that she had become increasingly nice toward me over the months we had worked together. I hadn't realized that I was becoming a substitute for the son she never had. She wanted to do something special for me on my birthday.

I was blind to the blessing someone receives when they give, and I hadn't thought about the impact my refusal of her gift would have on her. I was totally ego-centered on what people might think *of me* if I accepted a gift from a staff member.

With hindsight, I wish I had learned better the lesson my mother tried to teach me as I grew up: "Always show gratitude for what people do for you, son, by giving them a simple thank you."

The degree to which you've been unaware of the impact of your behavior on others probably correlates with the degree to which you are creating unnecessary interpersonal relationship problems and troubles for yourself.

As a person of intentional integrity, you'll take stock of your "impact quotient." Ask yourself, "To what extent would the people around me say I make a positive impact on them? A negative impact?

You'll find that your specific behaviors (what you think, say, and do) have a positive or negative impact on others in three primary areas:

- *Emotional*—the negative impact of your behavior can trigger in others emotions such as fear, anger, hurt, and frustration.

- *Attitudinal* —the negative impact of your behavior can trigger in others attitudes such as disgust, blame, resistance, and distrust.

- *Physical* — the negative impact of your behavior can trigger such things as stress, stomachache, headache, and backache.

Take time to assess any negative impact you're having on others. Having a general sense that your impact on others is either neutral, good, or bad is not good enough. You need to be able to describe in specific terms for specific people the *kind of impact* you are having on them and be able to connect the impact to specific behaviors you manifest in their presence. In that way, you can begin to make changes in your behavior that will allow you and others to benefit from the effect you *desire* to have on them.

SKILL 11: BEING REAL

This is a difficult attribute to describe. Like quality, you know it when you see it. Being real is essentially expressing congruence and naturalness.

When we interact with others, we have a sense of when a person is or is not "for real"—is or is not congruent and natural. The main cause of failure you'll encounter in this area comes from being overly concerned about being competent in some particular area. If you have concerns about competency, you may have fallen into the energy-consuming trap of trying to *play the role* of being competent, of showing off the *symbolic* aspects of competence while not possessing and applying the *substantive* aspects of competence.

Trying to be someone you are not doesn't fool anyone. Most people see right through us when we attempt it, and it's a low-integrity move.

The key to gaining and maintaining congruence and naturalness is to know when you're pretending to be something you're not. Given this insight, you can begin to identify the driving emotions (fear, anger, hurt) that are motivating you to pretend. As you describe them, you will be better able to dissipate them so that you can regain your congruence and naturalness. A process for doing this will be discussed in chapter 9 on peacemaking skills.

A signal that you may need to pay special attention to this skill is that you become irritated when people you trust tell you that you are not trusted. If you elect to solicit one or more persons to help you gain and maintain congruence and naturalness, be sure you enter the relationship in a climate of open, mutual inquiry. This is absolutely essential if you are to make significant progress toward discovering the truth about yourself.

SKILL 12: RESOLVING CONFLICT

Conflict is! The issue is not whether you have conflicts but how you respond to and resolve them. As an adaptive person you will be able to respond and work through conflicts rather than react to them. When you were a child you were caught up in many kinds of conflicts and developed preferred ways of dealing with conflict in general. As a result, you may find that you deal with all conflicts the same way. You may stand up and fight, run away, or ask for help.

An adaptive person develops an ability to respond to conflict with flexibility. Developing different conflict response strategies is an adaptive skill that will enhance the integrity with which you deal with conflicts and position you to gain greater balance in your life. It will also benefit the other people involved in the conflict.

The labels for the five response styles identified in the survey that follows were developed by Kenneth W. Thomas and Ralph H. Kilmann in the Thomas-Kilmann Conflict Mode Instrument. I recommend that you use their instrument to gain a more complete understanding of the concepts and a more accurate assessment of your conflict response preferences. The survey will help you gain a general sense of the response preferences you use to deal with conflict situations that emerge between you and your family members, your colleagues at work, and others. To validate your perceptions, I suggest that after you complete the survey, you interview your spouse or other family members and a colleague at work and record his or her perceptions.

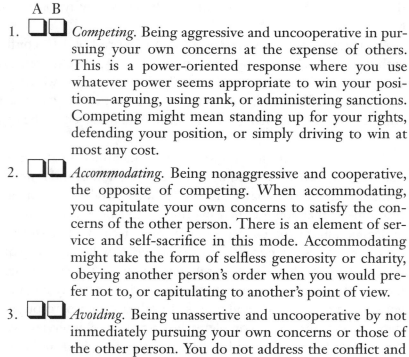

Time Out! *Complete the survey below.*
Reflect on your results.

Survey of Conflict Handling Preferences

In the "A" box in front of each conflict response preference, please mark the percent of time (10% low–100% high) you believe you use each in conflict situations at home or work.

Now interview another person you trust and in the "B" box mark the percentage of time he or she experiences you using each response preference. Discuss with the person the insights and observations supporting each other's perceptions. Listen actively with good eye contact, nonverbal nods and smiles, verbal acknowledgments, clarifying questions, and paraphrasing to show understanding!

A B

1. ☐☐ *Competing.* Being aggressive and uncooperative in pursuing your own concerns at the expense of others. This is a power-oriented response where you use whatever power seems appropriate to win your position—arguing, using rank, or administering sanctions. Competing might mean standing up for your rights, defending your position, or simply driving to win at most any cost.

2. ☐☐ *Accommodating.* Being nonaggressive and cooperative, the opposite of competing. When accommodating, you capitulate your own concerns to satisfy the concerns of the other person. There is an element of service and self-sacrifice in this mode. Accommodating might take the form of selfless generosity or charity, obeying another person's order when you would prefer not to, or capitulating to another's point of view.

3. ☐☐ *Avoiding.* Being unassertive and uncooperative by not immediately pursuing your own concerns or those of the other person. You do not address the conflict and might diplomatically sidestep the issue, postpone the

issue until a better time, or simply withdraw from the situation.

4. ☐☐ *Collaborating.* Being both assertive and cooperative, the opposite of avoiding. Collaborating involves attempts to work with others to find some solution that fully satisfies your concerns and theirs. It means digging into an issue to identify the underlying concerns of all parties and to find an alternative that meets both sets of concerns. Collaboration might take the form of exploring a disagreement to learn from each other's insights, deciding to mutually resolve some condition which might otherwise have you competing for resources, or confronting each other and trying to find the right solution.

5. ☐☐ *Compromising.* Being intermediate in both assertiveness and cooperativeness with an objective to find some expedient, mutually acceptable solution which partially satisfies both of you. It falls on a middle ground between competing and accommodating. When compromising, you "give up" more than when you compete but less than when you accommodate. Likewise, it addresses an issue more directly than avoiding but doesn't explore it in as much depth as collaborating. Compromising might mean you split the difference, exchange concessions, or seek a quick middleground.

SKILL 13: TAKING RESPONSIBILITY

When empowered with this skill, you will take full responsibility for your thoughts, talk, and actions. You'll not be bound up by the stress others experience because of defensiveness or being caught off balance when they have not covered their bases. You'll not blame others for the circumstances or difficulties surrounding you. You'll instead look inward to discover where your thinking and actions were off course or incomplete. You'll go 100 percent of the way to make things right and to do the right thing.

Assessment of Your Adaptive Skills

Please read the two polar statements for each category of adaptive skills. Then record your perception of your skill strength in the box at the beginning of each adaptive skill. Enter 1–5 for *very weak* to a *little weak* if the first statement is more true, or 6–10 for *some strength* to *great strength* if the second statement is more accurate.

1. ☐*Participating in Learning.* Seems unconcerned and uninterested in learning and improving. Or is highly concerned about quality performance and is voluntarily involved in personal learning and growth.

2. ☐*Responding to Legitimate Authority.* Responds in highly dependent or counterproductive ways. Or is interdependent and dependent or resistant when it is reality based.

3. ☐*Exercising Own Authority.* Is unable to give firm directions even when appropriate. Or is able to give orders with ease and seems comfortable with his or her own authority.

4. ☐*Communicating Emotions.* Does not express emotional states and never describes emotions. Or expresses emotions often and is able to describe them accurately.

5. ☐*Receiving Feedback.* Defensive and/or punitive when receiving feedback. Or receives feedback easily and easily gives it.

6. ☐*Giving Feedback.* Never attempts to give feedback or gives "dirty hit and-run feedback." Or gives descriptive "I" messages and is willing and able to deal with the reactions of others receiving them.

7. ☐*Facilitating Self-correction.* Seems closed to personal growth or change. Or solicits feedback and seeks growth.

8. ☐*Maintaining an Accurate Self-concept.* Seems grandiose or self-deprecating. Or has an accurate self-concept.

9. ☐*Adapting to Reality.* Overreacts to accolades and criticism from others. Or adjusts to a more realistic view with feedback from others.

10. ☐*Awareness of Impact on Others.* Insensitive to negative impact of words and actions on others. Or reads other people well and responds effectively to various situations.

11. ☐*Expressing Congruence and Naturalness.* Seems unreal. Talks one set of values and lives another. Or appears natural in various places. Verbal and nonverbal messages are congruent.

12. ☐*Resolving Conflict.* Avoids or overreacts. Or adapts to different styles when addressing each situation.

13. ☐*Taking Responsibility.* Will only go halfway at best and blames others for own failures. Or takes 100 percent action and owns problems and works to help resolve them.

After completing the survey, think about ways you can strengthen and employ each of the adaptive skills to help you find greater balance and alignment of each of the spokes on your wheel. Take sufficient time to record your thoughts, ideas, and growth goals in the appropriate sections of your notebook.

TIME OUT! *Reflect on:*
What? So What? and Now What?

Key Reflections

1. What are the attributes I need most to strengthen my adaptability?
2. How will greater adaptability benefit each dimension of my life?
3. When and how will I start doing it and who will help me?

TAKE A "WHEEL TRUING" TIME OUT!

Work on a spoke you haven't yet "trued."

Please turn to appendix A for guide questions.

9

PEACEMAKER SKILLS

Larry and Anita Reuland are peacemakers. By most folks' standards, they had it all. A loving marriage relationship, great children, an expensive home on the water with all the trimmings, a private jet, and more money than they could effectively spend. They had accumulated it all over the course of starting, running, and selling several successful business enterprises.

One day Larry bought a business that eventually failed. Anita had strong reservations about their buying it, but Larry went ahead with the deal anyway.

Looking back, Larry admits he didn't really know what he needed to know about the business when he purchased it. He admits that he ignored basic information and numbers that said "no go" on the deal. Admitting to arrogance and pride, he concedes that he had rationalized and convinced himself that because of his proven business acumen *he* could turn it around. He couldn't and didn't. As a result, the family fortune was lost. His advice to others? "Pride comes before a fall. Know God's Word and don't violate it!"

As Larry and Anita faced bankruptcy, their consciences told them their personal integrity was under fire and they needed to take time for a reality check.

With the help of prayer, pondering, and a right perspective from his wife, Larry and Anita made the intentional decision to be peacemakers instead of declaring war on their creditors. Instead of fighting through the situation, using the quickest and most financially expedient way out for them, they turned to good counsel. Their advisors helped them conduct an orderly liquidation of their business and fulfill their heartfelt desire to eventually pay all of their creditors—to do what was right.

Why would Larry and Anita take this alternative? Why not go for bankruptcy as some of their friends in business and at church suggested? Because Larry and Anita allowed their faith rather than their fear to dictate the parameters of their character. They felt they couldn't be a party to letting any of their creditors go down the tubes because of their bankruptcy while they retained their lifestyle at their creditors' expense.

In addition to liquidating the business, they chose to sell their home along with a considerable amount of their personal possessions to make peace with, and do right by, their creditors. Larry and Anita were eventually able to pay back the bank and all of their creditors.

They are now living a debt-free life. Their integrity is intact, they are guilt free, and both are very content. In the process of carrying out what their advisors called "orderly liquidation," they were able to keep peace with their creditors and made lots of loyal friends as well as business associates. Many of their creditors voluntarily reduced the amount owed them because they were so grateful Larry and Anita were trying their best to do right by them. As a result, Larry and Anita have positioned themselves as trustworthy persons and are now able to go back into business at any time.

Larry's affirmation and appreciation of his wife's love for him was special, "During and after the situation she didn't remind me of my mistake. She built me up as a man and has never thrown the situation back in my face."

Their commitment to be people of intentional integrity was summed up in a comment when Larry and Anita shared their story with me, "We won't maintain our lifestyle at the expense of jeopardizing the businesses of others."

The attitudes, skills, and knowledge for being an effective peacemaker are integral to managing your integrity. They will help you achieve and maintain balanced living. The skills described in this chapter are from the Peacemaker Series of workshops I developed to help Christian couples, parents, leaders, and students resolve and prevent recurring interpersonal conflict at home, school, and work.

I tried for years to correct the negatively conditioned, ego-motivated "should be, gotta be, and wanna be" thoughts I knew were stored in my subconscious mind. Some of them would come uncontrollably out of my mouth, and others would uncontrollably drive my negative emotional outbursts and verbal attacks.[11]

BECOMING A PEACEMAKER

Each of us faces situations that are laden with the potential for increasing or decreasing interpersonal conflict. The choice is always ours to make war or promote peace. As a person committed to intentional integrity at home and work, you are in an excellent position to model peacemaking. You can strengthen your own skills and facilitate the development of other's skills in resolving and preventing recurring interpersonal conflict. As John Calvin said, "We do not serve God unless we are in *any case* lovers of peace and are *eager* to promote it. Whenever there is a disposition to quarrel, there you can be certain God does not reign."

A loving peacemaker thinks, says, and does the right thing. This is the result of righteousness flowing out of a person who has received a "grace invaded, transformed heart." They have said, "Lord, change me!" and have accepted Christ as their *Lord and Savior*. Righteousness is an inside-out transformation orchestrated by God, not an outside-in work by man.

If you're not a Christian, my prayer is that you'll seek the truth for yourself about the saving grace of Jesus Christ from the Bible. Ask a Christian friend to tell you about Jesus and how He can change your life from the inside out.

TERMS

Law of Righteousness: Any action to ultimately achieve a correct result pleasing to God must be based on God's truth, commands, and moral standards for conduct.

Right or Righteous Action: Doing what God wants us to do by responding to the need of the situation appropriately vs. one's own opinion or ego-motivated desires.

Irrational Thought: Wrong thinking that, if formed in an emotional state, gets stored in the subconscious.

Negative Emotion: An internal reaction to something that activates wrong thinking, talk, and actions that lead to conflict.

Compulsive Demand Sentence: The words forming an inaccurate or irrational thought stored in the subconscious, defining the compulsion and the circumstance under which the compulsive thought is to be played out.

Reality: Whatever exists and happens as a result of God's natural, spiritual, and behavioral laws that have predictable cause-effect results.

Truth: A statement that describes God's reality that is beyond the opinion or judgment of a person or persons.

The survey below will help you assess your conflict prevention intention and strengthen your resolve to be a peacemaker.

Survey: A Peacemaker's Conflict Prevention Intention

In the "A" box please mark the degree (1 low–5 high) you *intend* to consistently manifest each of the traits of a peacemaker. In the

"B" box mark the degree you *actually manifest* each trait when engaged in conflict situations with others. Interview your spouse or another confidant and ask him or her to tell you their perceptions of the degree they experience you demonstrating the traits of a loving peacemaker when you are dealing with conflict situations or problems with them. As you interview them, record *their scores* in the "C" box and then explore together one another's insights as to the reasons for the similarities and differences in your respective scores.

A B C

1. ☐☐☐ Demonstrate *patience* when relating to others?
2. ☐☐☐ Express *kindness* toward others?
3. ☐☐☐ Show *gratitude for blessings* others bring you?
4. ☐☐☐ Demonstrate *graciousness* toward others?
5. ☐☐☐ Serve others with a *humble* spirit?
6. ☐☐☐ Demonstrate *politeness* in word and deed?
7. ☐☐☐ Demonstrate a value for *giving and serving?*
8. ☐☐☐ Express *calm understanding* during conflict?
9. ☐☐☐ Show delight in treating others with *justice?*
10. ☐☐☐ Bring God's *truth* to bear in all situations ?
11. ☐☐☐ Reach out to *forgive* others' mistakes and faults?
12. ☐☐☐ Work diligently to *protect* others' best interests?
13. ☐☐☐ Show *trust* in others?
14. ☐☐☐ Demonstrate *hope* in difficult situations?
15. ☐☐☐ Show that you *expect* the *best* from others?
16. ☐☐☐ Demonstrate *loyalty* to others?
17. ☐☐☐ Show *perseverance* in doing what's right?
18. ☐☐☐ Manifest *goodwill* in word and deed?

After completing this survey, schedule time with your spouse or other confidant to reflect on your intention to think, say, and do what is righteous to prevent interpersonal conflict and problems. Which of the exemplars of a peacemaker do you need to strengthen? In your notebook, list examples of what you presently do to express each exemplar in relation to the people you deal with in each spoke of your Wheel of Life.

TIME OUT! *Reflect on:*
What? So What? and Now What?

Key Reflections

1. What are you doing now to promote peace in your relationships?
2. What benefits can you expect from improving your peacemaking skills?
3. What growth goals and action steps do you need to address?

UNDERSTANDING RESISTANCE

We all experience resistance within ourselves and from others. It seems inevitable. However, it can be identified and overcome in ways that will help you more quickly and easily prevent conflict and resolve personal problems. First, you must deal with it rather than deny it. By dealing with it, you will better understand your motives and make adjustments that will contribute to your ability to think, say, and do the right thing.

The kind of "resistance" we'll be addressing is emotional in nature and centers on your reactions to others and events that keep you from satisfying your needs or wants in a given situation. It also includes the resistance you feel when you are confronted with information that challenges what you already think is correct.

Most of us resist taking responsibility for the conflicts and problems we experience. We don't want to look at what we are thinking, saying, and doing to bring both about. Taking responsibility creates feelings of vulnerability or loss of control.

Resistance manifests itself in both verbal phrases and nonverbal signals. As a peacemaker you need to be alert to both as you observe and listen to yourself and others.

Some typical phrases that indicate resistance is present are:

- "You don't know what you're talking about!"
- "I don't have the time to try anything new."
- "This is a ridiculous idea."
- "We tried that before and it didn't work."
- "We're already stretched too thin."
- "That sounds good in theory, but it's impractical."

Some typical nonverbal signals that resistance is present are:

- Tense vocal responses.
- Fatigue, absence from work, and illnesses.
- Indirect eye contact.
- Tense facial expressions.
- Angry and hostile outbursts.
- Avoidance of completing work.

Instead of thinking of resistance as something to be feared and denied, think of it as something that needs to be surfaced, analyzed, and used to help achieve truthful, rational thinking. As a person of intentional integrity, you will elect to surface and resolve your resistance. As you work to prevent and resolve interpersonal conflict and problems, you will use your resistance as a barometer for alerting you to the fact that one or more CDS (compulsive demand sentences) keep you from doing the right thing.

UNDERSTANDING FEAR

We observe others who are irrational and untruthful. However, most of us do not see the ways in which *we* are irrational and untruthful. What is more important, we don't like to be told about it!

Irrational, untruthful thinking is thinking that contradicts God's laws and commands. It weakens a person's conscience. It fosters wrong action based on faulty internal character and external conduct which leads to conflict and problems.

A key emotional motivator behind irrational, untruthful thinking is FEAR—**F**alse **E**vidence **A**ppearing **R**eal. It surfaces when we face people or situations that we think will cause us to lose control or experience vulnerability. Fear more easily takes hold of you when your conscience is weak. It cannot take hold of you when your conscience is clear and strong. To position yourself for resolving and preventing the interpersonal conflict and problems caused by irrational, untruthful thinking, you need to understand how fear works. You need to know how to gain a clear and strong conscience by surfacing and removing from storage the subconscious CDS that were built on lies and replace them with what is true and right.

The emotion of fear dissipates your faith and triggers your fight-or-flight responses. Fear surfaces when you are blocked in your ability to get what you want rather than do what is right, according to God's will, in a particular situation. The emotion of fear is the basis for all negative emotions. It manifests itself using a variety of masks—anger, hurt, blame, and frustration. Fear triggers thoughts, words, and actions that cause you to think, say, and do the wrong thing. You attack and defend.

One morning I was hurried as I showered and got dressed for a business appointment. Our son, Scott, asked me if he could back my car out of the garage to pull his in to clean and vacuum it. I said sure and I heard him back my car out of the garage while I was getting dressed.

As I was ready to leave, I didn't see my keys on the dresser. I yelled at Scott, "Where are my keys?" His response was, "I don't have them!" Then the attack and defend scenario began.

I was angry that I was about to be late for my appointment and verbally blamed him for not being responsible by putting my car keys back where they belonged. We bantered back and forth with blame and denial until he finally countered back angrily, and with a tone of hurt, saying, "You're calling me a liar! I used your extra car keys hanging on the key rack in the garage to back out your car!"

With this shot to the heart, and the recognition that I had wounded a person I loved so very much, I returned to my dresser. There were the keys! My worry and anger had led me to make false assumptions and accuse Scott. It blinded me to the truth.

As you and others go back and forth between attacking and defending, you will become more and more irrational and find yourselves going deeper and deeper into a pit of oscillating dysfunction and recurring conflict and problems.

When you are attacked, you'll usually feel defensive and find a direct or indirect way to counterattack. As with all defensive behavior, which is designed to keep the truth about the fear from our awareness, attack preserves the problem of compulsive thoughts, words and deeds.

Are you holding onto the belief that attacking can really benefit you? Are you aware that attacking and defending do not produce the results you deeply desire in your relationships with others? Both attacking and defending always produce wrong results because God's laws always prevail. Righteous action eventually gets right results; wrong action eventually gets wrong results.

Conforming to God's laws allows you to develop a clear and strong conscience that will give you a preventive stance as you face potential conflicts and problems. You'll be able to keep yourself out of the pit of oscillating dysfunction that is driven by fear. As you pray for the Holy Spirit to give you the strength and willingness to accommodate the righteousness God has already given to you through Christ and His grace, you will find your fearful perceptions dissipating as you recognize your irrational thinking; then you'll be able to rationally think beyond the FEAR or the False Evidence that is Appearing Real. As you pray for a clear, strong conscience, you will find that the Holy Spirit will help you align your thoughts, words, and actions with God's truth as you openly and rationally analyze each conflict situation.

SEEKING THE RIGHT SOURCE OF "TRUTH"

There are three sources of "truth" people use as the basis for making decisions. Only one source is proven and dependable. Let's examine them.

Self-made Laws —These are the "my" principles or "my" rules individuals form for themselves. As a kid, when the kids were playing at my house, I did it a lot of times. I changed the rules of a particular game to gain personal advantage. "House" rules!

TIME OUT! *Reflect on:*
What? So What? and Now What?

Key Reflections

1. In what parts of your life do find fear overcoming faith?
2. What are the benefits of knowing resistance is natural, understanding is critical!
3. What steps will you take to resolve your own resistance?

We form these kinds of rules based on our own limited knowledge and experience as well as our desire to justify our personal motivations and desires. One self-made law I find prevalent today is "Do it to others before they do it to you!" Another is "Convenience over commitment." The latter self-made law too often overrides the sacred marriage vows.

Legal or Culture-made Laws—These are the "laws of the land." They are initiated, theoretically, as a result of the "collective wisdom" of a society of people. In America federal, state, and local laws have been put in place by our elected representatives supposedly to protect us, guide us, and restrict our wrong actions.

God-made Laws—These are the laws established by God. Many laws regarding such things as righteous conduct, marriage relationships, the integrity of personal relationships, quality of work and the conduct of business are spelled out in the Bible in the form of standards, commands, admonitions, and directives. Others are observable physical laws such as gravity. The scientific community is in a continual process of discovering the physical laws God put in place at the time the earth was created.

THE IMPORTANCE OF RIGHTEOUS INTENT

In order to obey and benefit from God's law of righteousness, a change of basic intent and motivation is required. You must intend to move from your ego-centered motivations to a motivation to do, to the best of your ability, what is right according to God's commands and standards.

If we leave things to our own devices, our ego motivations will contribute to weakening our consciences and fostering undesired conflict and problems. When we fail to accommodate the character and nature Jesus has offered to us through God's grace, we begin capitulating to our ego motivations. I like Ken Blanchard's notion that when we go our own way we often end up **E**dging **G**od **O**ut of our conscience. We put ourselves in jeopardy of defiling and weakening it! *Maintaining a God-centered vs. ego-centered motivational focus is critical if you expect to gain the maximum benefits from God's law of righteousness.* You will be blessed when you adopt the simple intent (motivation) to do what is righteous in every situation of life. That basic motivational commitment is the key to resolving and preventing conflict in your life. A guiding question to help you stay on track is, "What would Jesus think, say, or do in this situation?"

RECOGNIZING AND UNDERSTANDING THE "VIRUS OF DISHONESTY"

The "virus of dishonesty" sits on our shoulders waiting to feed our egos. It tries with all kinds of rationalizations in an effort to divert us from acting on the standards for conduct God has told us to obey.

With diligence *beware!* The virus wears a coat of green woven with envy and greed. It has huge sharp teeth that bite deeply into your brain and heart and distort your conscience. It sits waiting on your shoulder each minute of each day, waiting for the opportunity to use its big red tongue and lips to whisper into your ear the great lie, "It's okay, it's okay, it's okay . . . EVERYBODY else is doing it . . . everybody else is doing it . . . why not you?"

A few years back my conscience brought me face-to-face with the virus. For years I had rationalized padding expense accounts and expenditures. Nothing I did had the potential of sending me to jail. I rationalized what I did by "saving" taxes and giving more than what I "saved" to church programs and worthy community causes. I further rationalized that I could spend the money I "saved" on taxes better than the people in government were doing. My concern over wasteful governmental spending was appropriate, but not using it as an excuse to justify my actions. I was clearly cheating and stealing. When I saw this, I stopped.

TIME OUT! *Personal Reflections*

How do you recognize the symptoms of dishonesty and their impact? They show up as wrong results. In addition to lying, cheating, and stealing, other examples are expressions of infidelity, guilt, defensiveness, defiance, addiction, fear, and excessive stress. Others are expressions of contentiousness, greed, anger, hatefulness, arrogance, and crookedness.

The list is by no means complete. Add to it.

1. List in your notebook the symptoms of the virus of dishonesty you see when you look at others. Also list those that are observable when you look honestly at yourself.
2. List the negative impact the virus has on your own and others' physical, mental, emotional, and spiritual well-being.
3. Select the symptoms of the virus you see in your home or workplace and discuss with your spouse or a colleague the negative impacts they are having.

EMOTIONAL FLAGS

Understanding your emotional flags is a starting point in the process of surfacing and eliminating the CDS (compulsive demand sentences) stored in your subconscious mind. Some of Albert Ellis's and Richard W. Wetherill's ideas are used in this section.

Like other people, you desire to get what you need and want. In your effort to satisfy your desires, you at times experience resistance in the form of "emotional flags." If you're like most people, when you are frustrated in your efforts to satisfy your needs and wants, you tend to react emotionally. At that moment what you do or say is less important than what you are thinking.

During those emotional experiences, you tend to talk to yourself, usually *not* aloud. However you do put your thoughts into specific sentences. Think about the examples below and substitute a familiar word or words in the blank.

"No matter how hard I try to . . . , you're never satisfied, so I won't ever do it again!" "I'll make you pay dearly if you don't . . . like I want you to!" "Forget it; I'll just fix the . . . myself and I'll never do the things you ask me to do for you!"

If you analyze these sentences, you'll see that each one is illogical and unrealistic. The sentence puts into words something you would consider untrue if you had been calm and thinking clearly.

Usually when you form such sentences, you have no sincere intention of following through on them. You soon forget your emotional outburst and assume that when you calm down your compulsive thoughts will just go away.

The problem is that your emotional compulsive thoughts do not go away; they get stored in your subconscious! The irrational, untrue thoughts remain in your memory bank just like programs stored on the hard drive of your computer. They also tend to retain the flavor and motivating force of the original emotion. The reason for this is that people overtly think with their conscious minds and do not understand the covert workings of their subconscious minds. After your conscious thinking has supposedly returned to normal, because your emotions have subsided, the original CDS still remain stored in your subconscious mind.

You can get rid of the conflict-producing irrational thoughts developed when you were emotional, by learning how to remove the illogical CDS stored in your subconscious mind.

ASSESSING YOUR MOST FREQUENTLY TRIGGERED EMOTIONS

This activity will help you clarify your main emotional triggers and the reactive thoughts, talk, and actions motivated by them. Please make two lists of up to five of the primary emotional triggers you experience in your day-to-day relationships according to intensity and frequency. The same emotional trigger(s) can be placed on both lists. You may list other triggers.

Typical Emotional Triggers

Angry	Hateful	Rebellious
Bored	Hurt	Rejected
Confused	Inferior	Resentful
Disgusted	Jealous	Sad
Dissatisfied	Judgmental	Shy
Frustrated	Lonely	Suspicious

MY HIGH-INTENSITY EMOTIONS

_____

_____

_____

MY HIGH-FREQUENCY EMOTIONS

_____

_____

_____

Finally, write down the main things you've thought, said, and done when you've experienced emotional triggers that are associated with conflicts with others.

Emotional Trigger	Thought	Word	Deed
_____	_____	_____	_____
_____	_____	_____	_____
_____	_____	_____	_____
_____	_____	_____	_____
_____	_____	_____	_____
_____	_____	_____	_____
_____	_____	_____	_____

TIME OUT! *Reflect on:*
What? So What? and Now What?

Key Reflections

1. What insights did you gain from identifying your emotional triggers?
2. What are the benefits of recognizing your own resistance and that of others?
3. What will you do to continue to discern your emotional triggers?

ELIMINATING THE CAUSE OF WRONG THINKING AND BEHAVIOR

Your brain traps and stores CDS. It was your wrong, illogical thinking tied to an emotional trigger that created your CDS in the first place. Understanding this and taking personal responsibility for the fact that you created them is critical. You add to your subconscious list of CDS each time you engage in recurring conflicts and suffer emotionally loaded interpersonal relationship problems.

Irrational thinking causes you to say and do the wrong thing and get the wrong results. It blocks from your heart the peace God promises to those who love and obey Him. Therefore, compulsive thoughts will not permanently satisfy the emotion that sparked them. The emotion does not fully subside, because the storage units in your brain cells do not empty. Instead they trap the thought and the emotion. Both remain available for repeated use on future occasions when the same emotion and compulsive thought is activated. The behaviors these emotionally driven, compulsive thoughts cause you to exhibit are as reactive as when you panic in fear and hit the brake as you notice you're about to drive through the red light at an icy intersection!

Consider the example of a man who thought this about his wife: "When she puts me down like that again, I'll smack her one!" Those words represent a burst of irrational compulsive thinking done in a flash of emotion. They cannot lead to action that satisfies the emotion behind them unless the compulsion is carried out. Therefore, the words are trapped in the subconscious brain.

The compulsive thought demanding action waits for the time when specific events activate it again. That time of renewed activation may never happen, but if his wife ever puts him down in the precise way that causes an explosion of the right degree of emotion, the husband will smack her one as predictably as he will react to a red light at the intersection of two icy streets by hitting the brake!

You can remove the CDS stored in your brain by using a release technique developed by Richard W. Wetherill. If you are like most people, you have done a large amount of emotionally loaded, compulsive thinking and have many subconscious CDS that cause various kinds of undesired compulsive behavior. When conflict arises between yourself and another person, you are faced with the difficulty of dealing with it. The good news is there is a proven process you can use to stop doing the things you keep doing *and don't want to do*—those things that cause recurring conflict and problems between you and others. Here's how it works.

You must reopen the closed mental storage units in your subconscious brain that contain the *CDS* that cause you to manifest the irrational compulsive thoughts that were stored when you did the original wrong thinking. You can reopen those closed storage units, but you have to know how.

Of course you can't reach into your brain and physically open those storage units, but you can open them through a clear thought process. When you think clearly you are opening storage units. In fact they are opening and closing all the time. The difficulty with overcoming past compulsive thinking is you don't open the proper storage units unless you know you should. Even when you know you should, when you first start to do it, you may resist! We all have strong urges to gratify our subconscious, emotionally driven compulsive thoughts and do not want to change them.

Learning to use a CDS elimination process starts by bringing your hidden CDS into view. Select any interpersonal conflict or problem you have with another person. Write down the subject of the conflict or problem and put your ideas related to the subject on a sheet of paper as fast as they come to mind. Each sentence should express the thoughts exactly, just as you have expressed them with emotion to yourself and others in the past. Remember, these sentences are all, or part, of some of your CDS, the precise wording defining the compulsion and the stated or implied circumstance under which the compulsion is to be obeyed.

For example, you may want to start with your thoughts regarding a conflict between you and another person about how money should be spent or saved. Write down the name of conflict, SPENDING MONEY, at the top of the paper. That's your subject.

Now list exactly what you have thought about the person, related to this subject, in the past. Do not edit your list or try to make it sound polite or rational. Write down *exactly* all the uncomplimentary, critical remarks you've thought to yourself or made to others about this person related to the subject you have in mind. The following sentences are typical though the gender may differ.

"He's the most wasteful, big spender I've ever known so I'll hide as much of our income as possible." "I could never trust him with managing a budget, so I'll do it and not let him see what we really have to work with." "He's always getting us into financial trouble and if he does it again, it's fire him or me!" "He always gives me a pain in the neck when I bring up our debt problems, so I'll give him as big a pain in his neck as he gives me!"

Sentences like these may seem extreme, but they are typical of the compulsive thinking we do when we are emotional. Some people do it virtually all the time.

It is irrational and wrong to form those judgments, because they get stored in your brain and influence your attitudes. They promote self-fulfilling prophecies. If you analyze the sentences honestly, you will see that they make no sense. Having parts of your brain storing compulsive thoughts about a person leaves you with a dysfunctional brain filled with trapped compulsions. Such compulsive thoughts will impair your thinking and cause you to be compulsively antisocial and show dislike and disregard toward others.

After the CDS are removed, you'll see virtues in the person with whom you've been in conflict. More important, your brain will no longer be disabled by the trapped, unrealistic, compulsive thoughts that magnified every fault and manufactured faults where none existed. In short, your thinking will become rational and truthful.

The way to remove your CDS is to inspect the CDS you've stored in your subconscious mind and see them for what they are: irrational, untruthful thoughts.

After you surface up to two dozen CDS about another person as it relates to a specific conflict, analyze them. As you analyze them, seek flaws in their rationality and truth. When you find and acknowledge the lie in a compulsive demand sentence, you have removed it from the storage unit in your brain and its power to continue to dominate your thinking. Cross it off your list, unless you still experience negative emotions when you read the sentence. If you do experience negative emotions, keep the sentence on your list for further analysis until you fully acknowledge it as a lie!

After the first reading of your list, add more critical thoughts as they come to mind. At first you can draw on your memory, then draw on your imagination.

There is a reason why this works. Many of your most damaging CDS were stored in your brain long ago. You cannot remember ever having thought them or having put them into spoken words. Therefore, they are beyond conscious recall.

The sentences you can remember thinking are easy to surface, but the sentences you cannot recall can also surface through your imagination. In your search for compulsive thoughts, your imagination tends to follow mental paths already established. If you have ever had a compulsive thought, you can think of it again. Actually you can think of it more easily than you could form a new compulsive thought. Therefore, when you draw on your imagination to extend your list, you tend to include the pertinent compulsive thoughts that seemed out of reach.

Some compulsive thoughts have a strong grip on your emotions. Notice and give a name to your emotional reactions when you look at your sentences to see how they are somehow irrational.

Try the process now. Begin the first step toward removing your CDS from storage and let God's truth about the situation fill you.

1. Collect on paper a list of your thoughts toward another person about a subject of conflict.

2. List exactly what you have thought about the person.

3. Inspect your CDS to see them for what they are—lies.

4. Add more critical thoughts as they come to mind.
5. When you find irrationality in one of your CDS and you do not react to it emotionally, cross it off your list.

TIME OUT! *Practice the Process*

You can intentionally engage in rational, truthful thinking and take a systematic set-of-action steps for gaining and maintaining equilibrium before saying and doing something wrong. Some suggestions are:

1. Set ethical guideposts.
2. Build high-integrity boundaries.
3. Recognize and label your "emotional flags."
4. Ask yourself, "What would Jesus think, say, and do in this situation?"
5. Maintain your intent to think, say, and do what's righteous each moment.

TAKE A "WHEEL TRUING" TIME OUT!

Work on one of the spokes you haven't yet "trued."

Please turn to appendix A for guide questions.

10

INTERPERSONAL COMMUNICATION SKILLS

I was sitting in Coco's, a local restaurant, waiting for my breakfast appointment to arrive. To my surprise he didn't show up. On a hunch I called the Coco's a mile away to check if he was there waiting for me. He was and I drove over to join him for breakfast. As we ate we exchanged the usual informalities and small talk.

When we got down to business, it was clear we each had a different agenda. I thought I was meeting with him to talk about my training program that helps managers hire winners. He was there to have me coach him through a personnel problem he was having at work.

What had caused us to get our wires so crossed? We had both heard the sounds coming from one another's voices over the phone, but it was evident that we had not communicated well. We had not come to a union of understanding. That's what communication is, a common understanding of the words and feelings expressed between two or more people. We had "broadcast" at each other and

141

had been guilty of selective listening because of our focus on our own agendas. Neither of us had truly listened to the emotional or between-the-lines verbal messages sent to one another.

The practice of active listening is a challenge for task-oriented people like myself. Over the years I've learned a lot about listening skills. I teach and coach others on applying them. I've practiced them and I get feedback from others on how I'm doing with them. Even so, listening continues to be a disciplined effort for me to do it actively and effectively.

I'm convinced that the most frequent problem people face at home and at work is poor interpersonal communication—failing to reach a union of mutual understanding, not necessarily agreement, with others.

I've found that my best ideas, plans, and suggestions are worthless if I fail to communicate them to other people effectively and if they don't listen effectively. The same holds true in reverse.

In homes, unnecessary stress, conflict, and wasted time is the result of poor communication. In American businesses, it's been estimated that poor communication adds up to billions in lost profits, opportunities, and employee productivity each year.

SEVEN "POSITIONING" PRINCIPLES

There are seven "positioning" principles that will help you get people to listen more effectively to you.

1. *Choose the right time.* You may be ready to speak to them, but are they ready to listen?

2. *Plan what you're going to say.* Think through what you want the other person to understand and do.

3. *Begin the communication process with a focus on the other person's needs.* Other people are deciding why they should listen to you. If you state how what you're going to talk about will benefit them, you'll usually get their attention.

4. *Listen first!* You'll get into trouble when you make assumptions like I did in my opening story. Try to get a fix on why the other person is there listening to you in the first place. Also try to determine their expectations for what they want out of the conversation.

5. *Say things positively and optimistically.* None of us likes to hear bad news, but it is important to state things as realistically and optimistically as possible. If you're talking about "bad news" stuff, say it in an up-front, factual, and nonpersonal way and quickly move into a constructive mode.

6. *Clarify one another's conclusions.* Summarize what's been said, be specific, and determine what's been decided and not decided.

7. *Close with an encouraging word.* Even if the conversation had some "fire" to it, try your best to end the conversation on a positive note.

We'll focus on two other interpersonal communication skill banks: *flexing your communication style* to accommodate yourself to the style of other people and *giving and receiving feedback* skillfully.

As human beings we are the dominant species on this planet because of our ability to communicate with words. Humans are the only creatures God put on earth that can talk themselves into conflict and trouble. After generations of practice, we have become good at it.

Think back over the last few days. Chances are you will find that at least some of your anxieties arose from situations where you did not understand what someone said, or someone did not understand what you really meant. In other words, effective communication was lacking.

Communication seems easy, but it isn't. It is so difficult that when you think about the many barriers to interpersonal communication, particularly those that are due to differences of background, experience, and motivation, it is a wonder that people can ever understand each other.

Communication is not one-way. It is not broadcasting. It is a two-way process. To be effective, communication between two people has to involve feeding information forward and feeding back an understanding of the information. This feedback reveals the degree to which a message has been understood, believed, and accepted. There will be misunderstanding. The goal is to anticipate a certain degree of misunderstanding and attempt to keep it at a minimum. The greater the number of persons involved in trying to communicate at a given moment, the more complex the process becomes.

Sharing and understanding is more effective when there is trust between you and the people with whom you're trying to communicate. Trust and communication increase when there is freedom from coercion and manipulation—when there is freedom to explore differences and when there is freedom from fear. People do not reveal their inner thoughts to anyone they fear. A person will communicate only what he or she wants the person to hear or thinks they want to hear. No genuine communication takes place.

What actions can you take to help build understanding and trust as you relate to others? The following principles serve as guidelines for effective communicative actions:

1. Be sure that communication channels are kept open. Probably the thing most damaging to interpersonal relations is for one person to not recognize that something is bothering another person and not being sensitive as to how they are feeling about it.

2. Make sincere expressions of appreciation and commendation to further interpersonal relations.

3. Never take credit for what another person has done, it can kill future communication efforts.

4. When others are doing things well, tell them so and give specific feedback on what is being done effectively. Communicating this fact gives people a feeling of accomplishment and satisfaction.

5. When appropriate, involve family members and colleagues at work in determining policies that impact them. Allow democratic discussion of group problems before a decision is made that will affect the group.

6. When irritating factors are brought to your attention, it is important to let the person know what is being done about the irritations.

7. Cooperatively planning with a person on how to carry out a particular task is better than simply issuing orders.

8. When working for the improvement of a person's performance, you should make known exactly what you observe them doing and what you want them to do.

9. Listen carefully to the viewpoints of others. One way to build relationships is to show that you respect others by listening attentively.

THE THREE R'S

I remember my mom and dad and some of my teachers admonishing me over and over again to master the three R's. They told me I would be "successful" in life if I mastered "Readin, Ritin, and Rithmatic."

They didn't, however, tell me anything specific about the three R's of Right Relationships:

- **R**ecognize the unique communication styles of other people.

- **R**egard others through how you treat them, talk to them, and talk about them.

- **R**espond to them in ways that best match their communication style and pace.

I found out through hard knocks that mastering the ability to acknowledge and respond to another's God-given personality attributes and communication style is tough. However, it's just as important, if not more important to success in life than mastering academic skills.

Communication and relationship skills help us build the trust and rapport that allow us to accomplish our individual and common goals together by getting quality work done in a timely way. My hurdle has been the diligent application of those skills at home and at work so that I consistently utilize my own and others' God-given personality strengths fully.

The PEOPLE Process™ kit contains a powerful set of easy-to-use communication tools for quickly determining my own and others' God-given personality type and communication style needs. The main tool in the kit is a colorful movable wheel that can be easily carried in your planner or briefcase. On one side of the wheel there is an opening that lets you quickly determine your own personality type and communication style as well as that of other people. On the other side of the wheel there is an opening that gives you specific behavioral clues for flexing your communication behaviors to respond to and communicate with others in the specific ways that will honor their personality type and communication style. These People Process tools were built on the forty years of research behind the Myers-Briggs Type Indicator.

Knowing and responding to people's natural personality type has helped me more easily and successfully influence and inspire them to do the right things. Loving, serving, and leading others at home and work toward achieving stronger character and competence—and faster, easier goal achievement—is being proactive. As you become knowledgeable and competent in the application of the communication tools related to personality type, you'll find interpersonal communication working more smoothly.

Consider these notions:

1. Every one of us—yes, even you—uses a blend of our personality types. No one is a walking pure type.

2. Despite using a blend or a mix, each person relies most heavily on a primary or dominant type.

3. An individual's lack of effective functioning or areas of behavioral difficulty often represent an overextension of his or her personality strengths.

4. People's personality type influences their communication style and is reflected in their behavior. Therefore it is observable and identifiable.

5. Personality types and communication styles should not be considered good or bad. Each type and style is unique and is no more right or wrong than any other.

What potential hurdles to effective and efficient interpersonal communications can these communication styles create? If you are a primary sensor you want to know immediately what I am proposing—what the bottom line is. If I am a primary thinker, and I insist on giving you the detailed run-down on my fact finding and historical review of the situation, we will not effectively interact.

You can learn to interpret your communication style more accurately and to interpret and assess the styles of others with whom you relate. You can also learn to temporarily flex your style to accommodate the style of another person. Flexing your style means communicating with another individual on his or her primary channel rather than communicating with all people as though they were just like you. Is this really possible? Absolutely! Is it easy? Certainly not!

Individuals rarely outgrow or discard their primary styles. In other words, a person's communicating style tends to be very stable through time. It would be difficult, if not impossible, for you or me to flex our styles continuously over a twenty-four-hour period. That is, if you are a primary thinker, it would be unrealistic for you to expect to be able to communicate effectively as a feeler for an entire day. However, most communicating is done over a much shorter time. How long is an average conversation with your spouse or child? One of your colleagues at work? A customer? Most people can, with practice, learn to effectively flex their style for limited periods of time.

Of course, flexing your style in itself is not the only key to effective interpersonal communication. Asking a person the right question can thaw a difficult communication transaction. For example, if you are dealing with a primary intuitor, ask him, "How do you feel about the idea we're discussing?" To a thinker, ask, "Based on your own analysis, how would you evaluate the relevance of the facts I've presented?" To a feeler, "I've given this idea a lot of consideration, but I'd like to know how you feel about it." To a sensor, "I hope I haven't bored you. What's your reaction to the idea?"

When you take the effort to learn to flex your style to accommodate the style of others, will they regard you as a phony? This is a common fear, but experience says no. People will say things like, "Now you're on my wavelength," or "I appreciate your being open enough to share some of your doubts and apprehensions," or "Thanks for boiling it down and respecting the fact that I really don't have a lot of time."

Give it a try. Practice both at home and at work and see if it doesn't make a difference in your effort to more quickly and easily balance the spokes on your Wheel of Life. Your decision to practice flexing your communication style, to become responsible for your own communication strategies, is a high form of caring, both for the message you are trying to deliver and for the person you are hoping will receive it.

RECOGNIZING AND RESPONDING TO OTHERS

The first step toward developing the three R's of Right Relations is to understand your own personality type and what works most effectively to get you to respond when people are attempting to focus your energy, help you process information, help you make a decision, and help you take appropriate action.

The behavioral clues from the People Process wheel are listed below. They will identify key behaviors to help you identify your own and others' types. Then you're ready to take the second step and select and use the appropriate response behaviors that are best suited to each person with whom you communicate.

Focusing Others' Energy

Recognizing Extroverts

Sociable
Outgoing
Expressive
Think out loud
Enjoy parties and gatherings
Like people interaction

Responding to Extroverts

Listen attentively
Be actively responsive
Be energetic and enthusiastic
Support their need to
    communicate
Recognize need for social
    interaction

Recognizing Introverts

Quiet
Dislike crowds
Talk one on one
Enjoy being alone
Entertain close friends at home
Keep thoughts private

Responding to Introverts

Relate one on one
Value their need for privacy
Allow them time to change focus
Ask questions to draw them out
Do not pressure for instant
    response

Helping Others Process Information

Recognizing Sensors

Factual
Realistic
Practical

Responding to Sensors

Be orderly and organized
Show facts with evidence
Be direct and to the point

Down-to-earth
In the "here and now"
Operate from experience

Draw on their experience
Be practical because they are

Recognize Intuitors

Conceptual
Imaginative
Enjoy new ideas
Future oriented
Consider possibilities
Look for meaning and purpose

Responding to Intuitors

Give them an overview
Have a vision of the future
Appeal to their imagination
Encourage their need to explore
Allow for the expansion of ideas

Helping Others Make a Decision

Recognizing Thinkers

Logical
Curious Analytical
Questioning
Prefer objective, rational approach
Seek knowledge

Responding to Thinkers

Expect and accept questions
Use logic
Be calm and reasonable
Be brief, concise, yet thorough
Present information for their
    analysis

Recognizing Feelers

Genuine
Harmonious
Compassionate
Make commitments
Base decisions on personal values
Relationship-centered

Responding to Feelers

Be honest and sincere
Be personal and friendly
Share with them your feelings
Encourage them to share their
    feelings
Allow them time to know and
    trust you

Helping Others Take Action

Recognizing Judgers

Decisive
Organized
Plan ahead
Set goals and meet deadlines
Accept responsibility
Prefer order and routine

Responding to Judgers

Don't disturb their order
Be prepared and deliberate
Value their time because they
    do
Finalize whenever and
    wherever possible
Take their deadlines seriously

Recognizing Perceivers	*Responding to Perceivers*
Flexible	Be open to options and changes
Adaptable	Use variety in your approach
Enjoy change	Let them set their own
Spontaneous	deadlines
Like to keep options open	Make use of their resourcefulness
Consider many avenues	Encourage possibility-thinking

A great way to master your style-flexing skills is to practice with some partners who have different types than yours. Use a three-person practice process. Have two people communicate on any given topic. Have the third person observe and record what he or she sees and hears. Then come together and conduct a reflective dialogue on what happened. Then rotate and do it again. Practice daily for a few minutes if at all possible and your mastery time will be reduced drastically.

Another strategy is to practice watching for the behavioral indicators of people's types as you watch television programs. See if you can determine their type by their behavior and what they say. Also see if you can tell when people on talk shows fail to communicate because they fail to flex their natural style to accommodate the style of the other person.

People can have fun with this convenient and easy strategy and also cut down their mastery time if they do it with a partner.

GIVING AND RECEIVING FEEDBACK

Giving effective, loving feedback to others will strengthen your communication impact on others. The following survey, based on research by the Kettering Foundation, will help you fine-tune your skills.

Survey: Feedback Principles

In the box in front of each feedback principle, please mark the degree, 1 low to 10 high, to which you see yourself effectively using each principle in the various dimensions of your life. In your notebook, list specific evidence to support your score for each principle. Also list what you believe you can do to enhance your scores. Ask others you trust to review your results and give feedback as to how accurate they think you are. As result of the insights you glean from the entire process, you may want to list specific personal growth goals related to one or more of these principles.

1. ☐ *Describe behavior rather than judge it.* When you accurately describe people's behavior to them as well as your personal reaction to it, you will leave them free to act on the feedback or not. By avoiding judgmental language, you will reduce the other person's need to respond defensively.

2. ☐ *Share both on-course and off-course behavior.* A balanced description of another person's behavior or actions includes both the constructive and destructive things they do in relationship to you. This gives them information for changing or maintaining their behavior to achieve the integrity and results they desire.

3. ☐ *Be specific rather than general.* A general statement about what another person says or does will not tell that person how to change actions that need changing or affirm when actions are appropriate.

4. ☐ *Address behavior others can do something about.* When a person receives feedback about behavior over which he or she has no control, it only creates resistance and an increased frustration level.

5. ☐ *Encourage others to solicit feedback, don't force it on them.* Feedback is most useful when a person asks for it.

6. ☐ *Check to ensure clear understanding.* What you intend to communicate is not always synonymous with the other person's understanding of your verbal and nonverbal messages. Ask the person what they heard you say. This will give you the opportunity to clear up any misunderstanding.

7. ☐ *Describe the person's behavior.* Rather than direct feedback at a person, include statements about the impact the person's behavior has had on you: your feelings, your personal effectiveness and efficiency in serving the other person, and other interpersonal relationship problems or issues.

8. ☐ *Give feedback immediately.* To maximize the usefulness and helpfulness of feedback, address the behavior right away

so the person can accurately recall what they specifically said or did. Then they are in a better position to evaluate their behavior and make a decision to modify it.

To increase these skills, you can use the three-person practice and reflective feedback strategy I described previously: two people practice the skills as they communicate about a given topic, the third person observes and records; and all three join together for reflection, dialogue, and feedback.

TAKE A "WHEEL TRUING" TIME OUT!

Work on one of the spokes you haven't yet "trued."

Please turn to appendix A for guide questions.

11

MUTUAL ACCOUNTABILITY SKILLS

Dave Baker made a tragic decision that took him from personal peaks to personal pits. Dave was an "All-American boy" destined for success. He was student body president in junior high, high school, and college. He was an Academic All-American and a basketball All-American at the University of California, Irvine.

After graduation he went on to play professional basketball in Europe and then to get his law degree at Pepperdine University. He was at the top of his class, joined a big firm, and went on to serve as legal counsel for the likes of Gene Autry and the California Angels.

Practicing law wasn't enough to satisfy Dave's drive for profit, power, prestige, and pleasure. He entered politics in Orange County and was elected to the city council. He became the mayor of Irvine—at that time the fastest-growing city in the United States. He was a guest speaker as often as six times in one day!

He had it made. He was selected citizen of the year for five years in a row and was practicing law in a prestigious firm of four hundred attorneys. At age thirty-four he was ranked number eight out of the ten most powerful men in Orange County.

Dave responded to an opportunity to run for the U. S. Congress against twelve other candidates. It was a tight campaign up to the end and very exhausting. It finally came down to "slime time."

A couple of days before the election the citizens received a mailer saying, "If Dave Baker's wife can't trust him, who can?" Though his wife, Patty, had campaigned beside him and had no cause not to trust him, the slime-slinging mailer hitchhiked on the tails of the Gary Hart and Jim Bakker incidents and successfully planted a lie.

Dave's campaign manager advised him that he had to counter with a campaign letter that very day and it would cost $40,000. If he didn't, he was likely to lose the close campaign.

As fate would have it, he and his wife had just refinanced their home and the money was coming the next day—$90,000—but he didn't have it *that day.*

Dave was the director of a foundation, and he decided to write out a check for $40,000 from the foundation, signing his name and the name of another director. He made it out to himself, thinking he could just replace the money the next day.

He turned in the check to the bank and went back to campaign headquarters. He told his wife about it without receiving any resistance because she had been under the gun with the "slime attack" too. As they talked, though, Dave's conscience told him he had done wrong. He went back to the bank forty-eight minutes later and got the check back before any funds had been transferred.

The next day he canceled all campaign efforts and closed down his headquarters. The following day he went to the board of directors of the foundation and told them what had happened and resigned from the board. He thought he had done what was right, given his wrong action.

He checked into a hospital to rest for three days, only to learn that the story had leaked to the press. Pressure was put on the district attorney, and Dave was charged with a felony. He agreed to plead guilty.

Because of that, he was suspended from the California Bar for two years. In the end, Dave lost more than an election. He lost his job, his profession, his home, the community he loved, and eventually his wife.

His family had to move from a big lake-front home to a condo. The continuing pressures and invasions from the press recording the family's new "lifestyle" was too much for Patty. As Dave declared, "She just couldn't take any more."

Dave contemplated suicide. One day while he was in the middle of the pit his son came to him and asked him to play catch. That brought him around. This began a four-year journey from darkness into light where God stripped away all the ambient noise that had been distracting Dave from a relationship with God and those he loved most, his wife and sons.

Through thought and prayer and the counsel of good men, Dave decided what he really wanted out of life:

- To have one specific relationship with a woman.
- To be a trusted friend to his boys as well as an authority and father.
- To have a few men in his life who could talk about something besides business.

As he reflected on his experience, he formulated principles he now shares with people when he tells his story. He committed to:

- live by priorities that reflect the values of his own choosing.
- live for the journey and the struggle, and to trust God and give over control to Him.
- live in the counsel of godly people he trusted rather than those who have their own interests in mind.
- focus on the important instead of the urgent, the eternal instead of the superficial.

Today Dave does his best to follow those principles and puts beans on the table by serving his clients as a brilliant attorney. He has paid back most of a $400,000 campaign debt. He commits enormous amounts of time to people one-on-one and to speaking at meetings and conferences to encourage people to do what's right according to God's standards for conduct.

His personal story about integrity under fire serves as a warning that what seems like a tiny slip can be a trip to the canyon's bottom.

It is also an inspiration to be a person of intentional integrity and to establish and maintain a PACT (Personal Accountability and Commitment Team) group. If Dave had been part of a PACT group as he entered the election battle, he would probably have sought their counsel and not taken the wrong action that caused such great losses and immense pain. The good news, however, is that he faced it squarely, was humbled by it, learned from it, and through God's grace has been growing into a more godly man ever since his fall.

MUTUAL ACCOUNTABILITY IS CRITICAL WHEN INTEGRITY IS UNDER FIRE!

One of the most life-changing mutual accountability processes a person of intentional integrity can put in place is a PACT. Some of the synonyms for the word *pact* are "agreement, alliance, arrangement, bond, compact, contract, and covenant." The PACT process incorporates all of these meanings. My PACT partners and I regularly challenge one another to ponder and individually declare whether our PACT agreement is still a covenant based on commitment or whether it has become one of convenience. We've found that a functioning PACT group *has to be built on a mutual covenant of commitment*, not convenience.

You can establish multiple PACT groups that may involve your spouse, just men or women, depending on your gender, other couples or your colleagues at work. A PACT will work in all these settings if the people involved are intentional about living out the values and standards for conduct they espouse. A PACT will work wherever you and others want to help each other better "walk the talk" by taking account of what you're each thinking, saying, and doing, and determining if it is right.

I like to think of accountability as the "ability to account" for my behavior and check to see if it contributes to the achievement of my stated vision, values, mission, and goals.

People who have clearly-defined operating values and who openly engage in a weekly personal accountability process with others have far less chance of capitulating to wrongdoing when their integrity comes under fire.

When you talk or profess one set of values and express opposite values at home or work, distrust and resentment will occur and your life will be out of balance. Getting involved in a PACT is a great way to align your talk with your walk.

FORMING A PACT

A PACT is an investment, and the process has a biblical foundation in Proverbs 27:17. "As iron sharpens iron, so one man sharpens another."

There are several arenas in which you can form a PACT. If you participate in a PACT in *all* of the arenas mentioned below *at the same time* you will experience POWER growth. It will take a huge commitment of time and energy, but you will certainly grow! A family PACT can be established with your spouse and also include your children who are seven years old or older. A family that initiates a weekly PACT process will find that every member of the family will grow in integrity and will strengthen each others' consciences, walk their walk more strongly, and more successfully navigate around the many chuckholes along the road of life.

The PACT process can also be established as part of any couples' Bible study group. The focus in this type of PACT is on the individual and the couple. Inviting couples you know, like, and trust from your church to form a group is a good place to start.

A more frequent way to form a PACT is to enlist a group of four to six people you know, like, and trust. Invite them to try the process for six months with the idea of evaluating it and then giving people the option of dropping out if it isn't working for them or meeting their expectations. I recommend these groups be made up of all men or all women, single or married.

A third arena to form a PACT is at work. Note, however, that colleagues participating in a PACT process within a given organization's culture are rarely as vulnerable with one another regarding personal and family matters. The focus of these groups is usually on individual integrity in the work and marketplace and on growing in areas related to personal and business ethics.

Most folks starting a PACT are more comfortable meeting with people they already know, like, and trust. Either way, there are key things you need to check out as you invite others to join you in starting the PACT process. All of them are related to commitment.

You need to verify face-to-face, before you formally start a PACT group, that you and the other people are sincerely committed to

- growth in integrity as a top priority personal-growth goal,
- making the PACT meeting a top priority,
- truthfully participating in the Integrity Check aspect of the process,
- being vulnerable and feeding forward mistakes to the group for help,
- openly receiving personal feedback from group members,
- receiving and giving coaching assistance to other PACT members.

Once you've gained the commitment of other people to establish a PACT, sit down together, reach agreement, and write out guidelines for your PACT. Here is a sample to help you get started.

Sample Guidelines for PACT Meetings

Our Purpose—To participate in weekly PACT Meetings with mutual accountability partners to help one another stand firm in thinking, saying, and doing the right thing.

Our Targeted Virtues—Self-Discipline, Compassion, Responsibility, Friendship, Work diligence, Courage, Perseverance, Honesty, Loyalty, Faith.[12]

Our Intent and Activities—Our intent is to support one another in strengthening a healthy conscience and good character. We want to be people of high integrity and virtue who more easily and regularly think, say, and do the right thing. The listed activities give us a flexible agenda that will be used to guide our activities during our PACT meetings. We want to achieve our purpose and at the same time help each other recognize and take the initiative to meet our own unique needs as we help one another live virtuous and reward-ing lives.

- Progress Reports—Celebration and sharing of our integrity success stories since our last meeting.
- Integrity Check—Responding to our key questions about "walking" our values.
- Coaching—As requested, conduct personal problem-solving dialogues and peer-coaching sessions.

MUTUAL EXPECTATIONS AND AGREEMENTS

- Commit to being mentally and emotionally present.
- Actively share personal thoughts, feelings, concerns, and needs.
- Actively listen to the thoughts, feelings, concerns, and needs of others.
- Maintain total confidentiality.
- Contribute to creating a safe, nonjudgmental meeting environ-ment.
- Be open to giving and receiving personal feedback and coach-ing.

TIME OUT! *Reflect on: Establishing one or more PACT groups.*

Key Reflections

1. What are the benefits from participating in a PACT?
2. What are the obstacles to establishing one or more PACT groups?
3. Who are the people best suited to be part of your first PACT group?

INTEGRITY CHECK

I and others have found the Integrity Check part of the PACT agenda to be the most threatening *and* the most growth producing. We've also found it to be the component of our PACT meetings that consistently helps members of the group stop short of doing wrong things. It keeps our consciences strong and alert to what is right and wrong. It helps us ward off the virus of dishonesty and thwarts personal rationalization.

Note that the questions are positive in nature. This is important. It puts the focus on what to do, not on what not to do. When you make your integrity questions positive in nature, it also allows you to easily convert them to a personal-growth goal for the week ahead when you've stumbled.

Sample Integrity Check Questions

I suggest each member of your PACT start a personal-growth journal. Encourage one another to reflect daily on personal actions and do personal Integrity Checks as part of a daily reflection time. Encourage one another to make notes so that each person can track and celebrate their improvements. Encourage one another to *focus on the vital* character goals that are most important right now!

Individually ponder and then share with each other, "To what degree (1 low–10 high) have I . . . How so? How not so?"

1. ☐ Been *self-disciplined* in terms of my words and actions?
2. ☐ Shown *compassion* by demonstrating understanding?
3. ☐ Shown *responsibility* by taking initiative in a timely way?
4. ☐ Extended *friendship* and a helping hand?
5. ☐ Done quality *work* joyfully and in a diligent and timely way?
6. ☐ Shown *courage* in conviction and action in doing what's right?
7. ☐ Shown *perseverance* in addressing my responsibilities?
8. ☐ Been *honest* by telling the truth and taking only what's mine?
9. ☐ Been *loyal* in word and deed?

10. ☐ Had *faith* over fear by doing what's right?

11. ☐ Not let *pride* or *fear* keep me from being truthful right now!

TIME OUT! *Reflect on:*
The content for your integrity check questions.

Draft a few integrity check questions important to you.

HELPING TO DETER
WRONG-DOING AT HOME AND WORK

There are six major steps you can take to put an Integrity Management process in place at home or work. They are:

1. Establish and communicate a clear statement of your family's or organization's vision, values, mission, and goals.

2. Determine the degree to which personal and group behavior is aligned with your stated vision, value, mission, and goals.

3. Identify the "toxins" in your family's or organization's culture that weaken the integrity of the key functions.

4. Establish clear program and performance goals to begin aligning personal and group behavior and outcomes with your intents.

5. Implement monitoring, feedback, and coaching strategies that involve all stakeholders in helping one another align performance with intents.

6. Establish an organization-wide ethics and performance accountability process that rewards ethical behavior and performance and corrects poor ethical behavior and performance from the top of the organization down.

As a person of intentional integrity who is committed to participating in and fostering mutual accountability, you will make a contribution toward turning around the present ethics crisis. With a solid PACT process in place in one or more arenas of your life, you will be more empowered as you surround yourself with people who are intent on being of good character and expressing good conduct.

An attitude of service and increased physical, emotional, time, and financial reserves through collaborative achievement is a direct result of people of high character, competence, and commitment living and working excellently together. If there is to be mutual accountability regarding the improvement of standards of conduct and performance, it needs to start with the adults in your family and at the top of the organization where your work. Accountability must be based on specified standards for performance as well as a set of standards for conduct that can be used to determine ethical and unethical behavior and competent performance. In your workplace, it is best supported by an organization-wide PACT process that encourages all participants in the various departments of your enterprise to more effectively "walk their talk."

TAKE A "WHEEL TRUING" TIME OUT!

Work on a spoke you haven't yet "trued."

Please turn to appendix A for guide questions.

12

CHANGE FACILITATION SKILLS

I became a school principal after serving in two wonderful positions. For several years I served as a demonstration and training teacher at a premier demonstration school. I had "been there and done that" in terms of helping difficult kids learn effectively. Following this assignment, I became a district-wide curriculum consultant. As a consultant, I could effectively diagnose learners and the learning environment and point out specific deficiencies in any educational delivery system. I was also skilled at prescribing instructional changes that would enhance the learning process for students and was skilled at coaching both principals and teachers.

What I didn't possess was the knowledge or skills needed to move people through the change process and effectively deal with their resistance to change. One day my lack of this knowledge hurt me.

I had hired in to a new district as a principal. When I started initiating major changes in instructional expectations for the staff, the heavens fell in. The end result? They gathered their political support and ultimately ran me out of town!

My motives and credentials for building a high-achieving, high accountability instructional program were impeccable. What I wanted to do was absolutely right for the kids in the school. I had complete board and superintendent support because they had hired me to strengthen the school instructionally. However, the teachers were comfortable and entrenched in the ways they had been teaching. No one had held them accountable for delivering first-class instruction, and they felt threatened and vulnerable when I arrived at "their school."

I tried to address the resistance logically and intellectually. I presented all the research, the success stories from other schools, and all the other information I could to help them understand why they needed to change and cooperate with me as I helped them change.

My efforts did little. I faced a staff with emotionally high levels of concern and resistance and I didn't know how to deal with it effectively. Thankfully, I do now.

MAKING CHANGES

There are key attitudes, skills, and knowledge you can possess to help you better respond to and/or orchestrate worthwhile changes.

A basic attitude that has helped me has been to recognize the reality that change is always happening. There are times when changes need to take place in your family or at work. Hopefully they will be well planned. Hopefully they will be executed in a timely and skillful fashion. Hopefully they will be worthwhile and in the best interest of everyone.

As you begin to think about any kind of significant, worthwhile change that needs to take place in your family or workplace, be aware of how the change will impact others. In your home or in your workplace, a new vision and new operating values constitute significant change. So do new performance standards, new policies or procedures, a new computer equipment installation, or a relocation of your home or business place.

INTEGRITY UNDER FIRE

When we make low-integrity decisions by initiating changes without thinking through the consequences, strategy, and timing, we can get ourselves into deep trouble! With God's grace and help, we can also turn bad decisions around and stand firm on the right ones! The ideal is to prevent the implementation of wrong decisions and changes and facilitate the right ones.

Judy Venn's story is a shining example of the above truths. Judy is president of Judy Venn and Associates, Inc., in Newport Beach, California. Her company is one of the largest agencies providing hostesses, hosts, costumed characters, sales assistants, crowd gatherers, translators, and demonstrators for all types of conventions in the United States.

Judy had been raised a Christian. At fifteen, with her seventeen-year-old boyfriend, she found herself pregnant. She married Ted, the father of her child, and later started a career in modeling and TV commercials. By twenty-five she was successful in her career and dissatisfied with married life. She filed for divorce, moved to Redondo Beach, California, and accepted a receptionist job to support her children.

Her husband, Ted, never gave up hope that they would get back together, even when he found out that Judy was dating other men. Ted did all he knew to do to get Judy to see his side of things regarding the restoration and raising of their family.

A month or so before the divorce was final, Judy felt God speaking to her. She responded, *"Lord, what have I done?"* Her thoughts were filled with *"Call Ted, call Ted and get back together!"* She called him and found out he had been dating and had proposed to another woman. The vision she had of the mistake she had made and the need to restore her family held strong. She asked Ted if they could get together and talk. They did, and from that point they courted again and in time reunited.

Judy wanted to use her talents to start an agency for trade show hostesses and presenters. She and Ted prayed about it and Judy's company was started. She had decided it was to be a company with high standards. She wanted her business to honor God and wanted to do all she could to make a difference in the industry's attitudes and actions toward women, particularly beautiful women who were representing companies on the trade show floors of America.

"Act like a lady and you'll be treated like a lady" was her motto. She also told clients that her people would not wear anything not in good taste. She refused to put anyone on the floor of a trade show wearing anything she wouldn't wear herself. The reputation of the quality of her firm drew large amounts of business. She received numerous Convention Bureau referrals and has set and raised the standards for the industry.

Judy is grateful for what God has done in her life. From the beginning of her business she and Ted concurred that the "fish" emblem had to go on her business cards and stationery because Jesus was her partner.

Has she lost business by letting people know who her partner is? Yes. When in the middle of firming up one of her biggest official provider contracts she had ever had, she was asked what the fish was on the order forms. They asked her to remove the emblem and she told them she couldn't do it.

The vice president of the organization called her and said they really wanted her to do the job because she had the best agency. He asked her to reconsider and pointed out how much money was involved. His basic message was that they didn't want to mix religion and business. Judy didn't agree and lost the contract.

In the long haul, it never affected her business. In fact, her company did a significant amount of business with that particular show. Judy felt good about her decision and believed God would honor it. He did.

KEY POINTS ABOUT INITIATING CHANGE

The following guidelines will help you prevent your family, career, or organizational "ship" from veering dangerously off course or sinking because of poor planning and execution of changes.

1. Involve those who need to help carry out the change in planning the change.

2. Clearly define people's roles in the change, the goals of the change, and the achievement indicators.

3. Transmit the goals and objectives for the change in writing to all responsible for helping implement the change.

4. Address people's needs! Disrupt only what needs changing to accomplish your goals. Retain the best of what is being done to get you where you're going—things like friendships, famil-

iar work setting, personally preferred work procedures, and group norms.

5. Design flexibility into the change process. Don't redirect your course too quickly or people may panic and your ship might hit some rocks and sink! Allow people to complete current efforts and take adequate time to assimilate new skills, procedures, support mechanisms, and work behaviors needed to successfully make the change.

6. Be open and honest with everyone affected by the change. Don't pretend that negative aspects don't exist.

7. Look for areas of agreement between yourself, as a leading orchestrator of the change, and those who oppose it.

8. Whenever possible, focus on the positive aspects and benefits of the change.

9. Establish parameters and define the limits of the change.

10. Design adequate training and allow mental and emotional adjustment time for the people involved.

11. Recognize your own limitations.

WHY PEOPLE RESIST CHANGE

Most people have anxiety about change. It's normal. When changes are being initiated, resistance will surface. You can count on it! The goal is to channel it and manage it toward helping people grow and go to new levels of excellence and service.

As I've coached people in the use of a proactive change process, I've helped them address many different kinds of change goals. As they've asked me to help them understand why they were having trouble orchestrating what appeared to be worthwhile and necessary change, I observed one or more of thirteen common causes of resistance in the people who are being impacted by the change.

1. The new goals and benefits were not accepted by the people who had to deal with and/or implement the change.

2. The reasons for change were not adequately or effectively communicated, nor were the benefits.

3. People feared the unknown and couldn't predict the outcome.

4. People feared failure.

5. People liked the current situation.

6. The purpose for change was not clear or relevant.

7. People disliked the person recommending, announcing, or implementing the change.

8. People saw the change as an attack on their performance and reacted defensively.

9. The timing of announcing the change was wrong or perceived as wrong by the people involved in it.

10. The belief that the change would make the boss look good, not them.

11. Fear of having to work harder because of the change.

12. Fear of loss of rights or status because of the change.

13. Resistance to change because it is change!

As I've observed people in the middle of chaotic change efforts, I've recognized that the change was not being planned or orchestrated well by the leader. As a result, I've observed people's resistance turn into defensiveness and even toxic attack!

It is tough to stabilize situations where people sabotage, emotionally blow-up, steal from the organization, and exhibit aggressive, overt resistance with blaming and finger pointing; where they moan and groan, withhold support, and fence sit; where they give fake agreement but behind the scenes show no initiative or commitment to making the change happen.

HOW TO AVOID THE PITFALLS OF UNSUCCESSFUL CHANGE EFFORTS

You can skillfully avoid surfacing toxic behaviors from others at home and in your workplace. At home, toxic behaviors create stress and obstruct the expression of love. At work they kill productivity, restrict cash flow, and reduce profitability.

Gene Hall and his colleagues when he was at the University of Texas, Austin, identified two critical pieces of information needed when a person is trying orchestrate changes that require the involvement of other people. They are the stage of concern people have about the new change and the level of use or prerequisite knowledge and skills they possess for supporting and successfully implementing the change.

CHECKING FOR CONCERNS

I particularly want you to know about the critical issue of people's concerns when it comes to change.

When you determine each person's stage of concern about implementation of the change you want to see happen, you'll prevent the "ship" you're guiding from crashing or sinking!

Each person you need to involve in the change is in one of these stages. A person's concern can flow in either direction from their main stage of concern, but it is the main stage that must be accurately identified and to which you must initially respond.

A simple, informal interview process usually uncovers where people are. As you talk to people, listen to what they say and get in touch with the emotions they are expressing through nonverbal language. If you read them right, you'll be able to place them in one of the stages below and then respond to them appropriately.

1. *Awareness*—The person exhibits little concern about or involvement with the change.

2. *Informational*—The person has a general awareness of the change and interest in learning more detail about it. The person seems to be unworried personally and is interested in the substantive aspects of the change.

3. *Personal*—The individual is uncertain about the demands of the change, personal adequacy to meet those demands, and personal role with the change. This includes analysis of his/her role in relation to reward structure of the organization, decision making, and consideration of potential conflicts with existing structures or colleagues.

4. *Managerial*—The person's attention is focused on the processes and tasks of implementing the change and the best use of information and resources. Concerns are related to efficiency, organizing, managing, scheduling, and time demands.

5. *Consequence*—The person's attention focuses on impact and relevance of the change on outcomes in his/her immediate sphere of influence, including performance, competencies,

and adjustments needed to increase employee and organizational effectiveness.

6. *Collaboration*—The person's focus is on coordination and cooperation with others regarding implementation of the change.

7. *Refocusing*—The person's focus is on exploration of more universal benefits from the change, including major additional changes.

TIME OUT! *Reflect on: What? So What? and Now What?*

Key Points

1. What worthwhile changes do you want to initiate?
2. What benefits do you see from orchestrating vs. *reacting* to change?
3. What action steps will you take to *proactively respond* to change?

TAKE A "WHEEL TRUING" TIME OUT!

Work on the last of the spokes you haven't yet "trued."
Please turn to appendix A for guide questions.

Part 4

MAINTAINING LIFETIME INTEGRITY

13

MAINTAINING YOUR "TRUING" PROCESS

Hopefully by now you've completed the working draft of your written plan for gaining and maintaining balance within and between each of the various dimensions on your Wheel of Life. You've explored strategies for incorporating intentional integrity into all the areas of your life. You've aligned your values with God's.

As you repeat the "truing" process throughout the rest of your life, keep your eye on your hub and your spiritual spoke! Your spiritual spoke being "trued" with your life purpose, vision, and values sets you up for balancing your entire Wheel of Life.

AN ENCOURAGEMENT TO NONBELIEVING READERS

If you've read through this book and you're not a Christian, I encourage you to look openly and seriously into the present and eternal benefits of becoming one. If you apply the concepts and tools in this book, they will make your life better. They will help strengthen your integrity in many ways. However, they alone will not help you build the life of integrity and balance you desire deep in your heart. You can only gain the maximum benefits if you have a personal relationship with Jesus Christ.

This is because Christ's Holy Spirit fills and guides Christian believers. His Spirit builds them up and fills them over their lifetime here on earth with Christ's character and nature.

What happens to you for eternity depends on your decision to accept or reject Jesus as your personal savior. When you die, it is too late to make that choice.

If you haven't made this important decision, I encourage you to read through the New Testament of the Bible. The Book of John is a good place to start. Find a mature Christian, someone who can help you clearly understand who Jesus is, understand the credibility of the Bible, the work of Jesus Christ, and how you can have eternal life in Jesus Christ.

AN ENCOURAGEMENT TO FELLOW BELIEVERS

As you engage in the "truing" process with an eye on the hub of your Wheel of Life and your spiritual spoke, keep in mind Jesus' warning in Matthew 6:24; "No one can serve two masters. Either he will hate the one and love the other, or he will be devoted to the one and despise the other. You cannot serve both God and Money."

He also told us in Matthew 6:31–33, "So do not worry, saying, 'What shall we eat?' or 'What shall we drink?' or 'What shall we wear?'

For the pagans run after all these things, and your heavenly Father knows that you need them.

But seek first his kingdom and his righteousness, and all these things will be given to you as well."

"Kingdom seeking" is an inside-out heart issue fulfilled in our relationship to Christ. When we honor Him as Lord, the fruits that come from our growth in Him relate directly to our efforts to be persons of intentional integrity. God's standards for high-integrity living are explicit in His Word. When we intentionally do what He says, we are seeking His kingdom here on earth, a personal sense of His peace, enjoying right relationships, and taking right actions that please Him. The result is called joy.

Henry Blackaby's and Claude King's tapes and book, *Experiencing God*, explain how we can find out where God is working in the various dimensions of our lives and join Him in that work and in experiencing Him doing through us what only He can do! I highly recommend it to you!

There are four things I do to discern if I am doing the things God wants me to do.

- Check to see if my mission, goals, and objectives for each dimension fit my natural style, personal history, and family needs.

- Check to see if each is in accord with Scripture.

- Check with my wife and PACT partners for substantiation.

- Check to see if my head and heart are both in a state of true peace. No ego highs, no emotional weight, just peace. (Matt. 11:29–30, "Take my yoke upon you and learn from me, for I am gentle and humble in heart, and you will find rest for your souls. For my yoke is easy and my burden is light" is what I use as a litmus test on this one!)

THE IMPORTANCE OF PERSONAL COMMITMENT

God promises to complete the good work He's started in you. What a partnership! One of the most inspirational quotes I've come across on the importance and power of personal commitment is from Johann Wolfgang von Goethe. It centers on acknowledging and trusting that God's wisdom and power will surround you, guide you, and provide for you as you pursue worthwhile and righteous goals for living a life of intentional integrity.

Until one is committed, there is hesitancy, the chance to draw back, always ineffectiveness. Concerning all acts of initiative and creation, there is one elementary truth ignorance of which kills countless ideas and splendid plans: *The moment one definitely commits oneself, then providence moves too.*

All sorts of things occur to help one that would never otherwise have occurred. A whole stream of events issues from the decision, raising in one's favor all manner of unforeseen incidents and meetings and material assistance, which no man could have dreamed would have come his way.

Whatever you can do, or dream you can do, begin it now. Boldness has genius, power and imagination in it.

Begin it now.

With a written draft of your life plan in hand, you can use the tools in this book to implement your established life purpose, vision, and values, as well as the specific mission, goals, and objectives you've established for the different dimensions of your life. Your commitment to carrying out the assessment and alignment process will be a continuing, lifelong process if the balance you desire in your life is to be kept at peak level.

I encourage you to commit to a thoughtful and comprehensive assessment of your Wheel of Life at the beginning of each new year. I've found that twice a year is even better!

If in between your annual or semiannual checkup your stress is up and you sense your life is not as balanced as you would like for it to be, go through an assessment and alignment process for the specific spokes you sense are out of balance.

FIGHT AGAINST THE TEMPTATION TO GIVE UP!

Grace and peace be yours in abundance through the knowledge of God and of Jesus our Lord. His divine power has given us everything we need for life and godliness through our knowledge of him who called us by his own glory and goodness.

Through these he has given us his very great and precious promises, so that through them you may participate in the divine nature and escape the corruption in the world caused by evil desires. For this very reason, make every effort to add to your faith goodness; and to goodness, knowledge; and to knowledge, self-control; and to self-control, perseverance; and to perseverance, godliness; and to godliness, brotherly kindness; and to brotherly kindness, love.

For if you possess these qualities in increasing measure, they will keep you from being ineffective and unproductive in your knowledge of our Lord Jesus Christ.

—2 Peter 1:2–8

Nothing in the world can take the place of persistence. Talent will not; nothing is more common than unsuccessful men with talent. Genius will not; unrewarded genius is almost a proverb. Education will not; the world is full of educated derelicts. Persistence and determination alone are omnipotent.

—Calvin Coolidge

Most people I know who commit to being persons of intentional integrity are just ordinary people with an extraordinary amount of true wisdom and determination. They just don't quit. They "keep on trucking."

Greatness is not going to be determined by your prestige or profits but rather by what it takes to discourage you. You can tell a lot about where you are by how you respond to failures and criticism from others. It reveals your character.

You might ask, "What will it take to discourage me from pursuing my life vision, values, mission, and goals when things don't go my way? When my expectations are not met? When someone disapproves of how I do something?

The worthwhile things that last often require more time and determination. God makes a fully mature oak tree in about sixty years. He takes about six hours to make a mushroom. I'd prefer to be an oak tree.

Galatians 6:9 will give you encouragement to build a life like an oak. "Let us not get tired of doing what is right, for after a while we will reap a harvest of blessing. If we don't get discouraged and give up."

PREPARE AN ANNUAL REPORT

I've used an "Annual Report" form my friend Bob Shank gave me as part of my check-up procedures. It is developed from the perspective that God owns me and is Chairman of the Board for the enterprise I call "my life." I make out the report as CEO to see how effectively I have kept the spiritual spoke on my Wheel of Life aligned and how well I have tightened the other spokes.

Personal Assessment for Preparing "Annual Report"

1. *Make a graphic of results and losses*—(Luke 2:52) Show your peaks, valleys, and plateaus.

- *Assess increase in wisdom*—(James 1) Wisdom is information screened through *compassion and experience*. It comes from the learning that takes place when your "wheels come off."

- *Assess increase in stature*—It's the way the world sees you, your reputation built over years, and your presentation of yourself. It can be destroyed with a bad decision.

- *Assess increase in favor with God*—(Matt. 17:5) Is God pleased with you? If not, what do you need to do to please Him?

- *Assess increase in favor with men*—(Acts 2:46) How have you related to people?

2. *Assess asset inventory and mix*—(Luke 12–15) Life success is not determined by abundance of possessions. Are you working harder for less eternal return? Is your warehouse full of worthwhile inventory inside yourself?

    - *Fitness* —How strong is your integrity and character? Fitness is the quality of the person we allow ourselves to become. Have you satisfied obligations before accommodating your own vices? What does the inventory in your internal warehouse look like?

    - *Attitude*—Have market conditions diminished your attitude or are you of the same attitude as that of Jesus Christ who made Himself nothing, just like us!

    - *Commitment*—How long do you hang on after something is not "fun" anymore? You can't tell how committed you are when things are good, only when things get tough! Is your commitment up and down? Are you on people's "watch and see" lists because they are not sure they can count on you?

    - *Training*—Are you benefiting from the unique educational opportunities to be found in your problems? Are you studying and applying God's Word daily? What was your greatest learning this year?

    - *Significant relationships*—These are forged in the fox holes of life and are mutually beneficial. What are yours?

3. *Assess your personal financial statement*—Do you know your bottom line or are you in a state of denial? If you were God, who owns (1 Cor. 6) "You Incorporated," would you sell off, keep, or close down the company? Why? Why not? Can you effectively live life when in down side as well as up side cycles? Do neither poverty nor riches pull you out of right relationship with God? Influence your ethical standards for conduct?

   - *Gross revenues*—(Prov. 30:7) Are they consistent and stable? Not too rich, not too poor?
   - *Overhead expenses*—(Prov. 24:27) Are you wrong-sized, right-sized or need to downsize?
   - *Capitalization*—(Luke 12) Having too much is a problem in God's mind. Having too little is a problem in your mind.
   - *Debt load*—(Rom. 13:8) Do your liabilities exceed your assets, according to God's accounting, or do you have net dividend income? Leverage is not king! The borrower is slave to the lender.
   - *Bottom line*—(1 Cor. 6) Has God received an ample return as an owner and investor in you?

4. *Make next year's forecast*—Think about these spiritual principles:
   - You are not your own! You were bought with a price!
   - Where your treasure is, that's where your heart is.
   - Do your giving while you're living, so you'll know where it's going.

AFTERWORD

I have a vision for *Intentional Integrity*. I picture a revived America! I see lots of people in all walks of life reading the book. I see them making a decision to *be* persons of intentional integrity. I see each of them growing and mastering the skills that will empower them to effectively "align" each spoke on their Wheel of Life with biblical values. I see them taking personal integrity seriously and modeling it for one another and their children.

I see leaders in churches, schools, businesses, professional services, government, sports, and entertainment talking to their colleagues and employees about the book as they promote and encourage an operating paradigm of intentional integrity and challenge the present-day paradigm of conditional integrity.

Like waves hitting the beach and stirring and smoothing rocks and particles of sand, I see increasing numbers of people turning their lives around and thinking, saying, and doing the right things according to God's standards for conduct. I see them helping others do the same.

I also see more and more people knowing Him and living their lives as if He truly is Lord of their lives.

As an integrity champion, you can contribute your part to bring this vision to fruition in your home and in your workplace. As you do it, I'd love to hear about your success stories. I'd also love to hear about your stories of "integrity under fire." I'd love to hear how you've stood strong in the face of the virus of dishonesty. I'd love to hear how you've tripped, fallen, picked yourself up again, and charged forward with intent, knowing you are a loved child of God and that you are doing all you can to be a person of intentional integrity.

Won't you drop me a note?

Millard MacAdam
ProActive Leadership Consulting & Training
2114 Vista Laredo
Newport Beach, CA 92660
Email: mnmacadam@aol.com

APPENDIX

SPOKE "TRUING" GUIDELINES AND QUESTIONS

The Wheel of Life highlights ten areas of life. This book gives you an opportunity to assess your current alignment in each area. As you assess your balance, the principles of Personal Integrity Management will help you discover ways to improve each area of life.

First, decide which spoke needs attention.

• Spiritual Growth	• Financial
• Intellectual Growth	• Physical Fitness
• Career Enhancement	• Social
• Community Service	• Family
• Recreation	• Emotional Growth

Next turn to that spoke in this appendix. The questions will help you think through what you want to include in your mission, goals, and objectives for that spoke. Make a copy of the questions related to the spoke and keep it available in your journal as you focus on developing your mission, goals, and objectives for that dimension of life.

Also look for creative ways you can apply the integrity management tools and strategies to help you keep this spoke functioning well.

When you complete the book and have a first draft for the vision, mission, and goals, for each of the spokes on your Wheel of Life, you can then return to this appendix and select any spoke you want to check and make "true" if you find it giving you a bumpy ride.

Spiritual growth is related to your growing knowledge of God and your intimacy and relationship with Jesus Christ. It is the increased fruit that is being produced through you as a result of loving and obeying Him. It is seeing where He is working and then joining Him in His work.

The following questions will help you think through what you want to include in the mission, goals, and objectives for the *Spiritual Growth Spoke.* Make a copy of the questions and keep it available in your journal as you focus on developing your mission, goals, and objectives for this dimension of your life.

1. What will spiritual fulfillment look like from my perspective? Is it compatible with God's perspective?

2. What types of spiritual objectives and activities will help me mature in Christ?

3. What can I do to develop and broaden my spiritual growth?

4. What steps do I need to take to accomplish my spiritual objectives?

5. How will I know my spiritual objectives and activities are contributing to a more balanced and beneficial life?

6. How will I know that my spiritual objectives and activities are the highest and best use of the emotional, physical, time, and financial reserves God has given to me?

My Spiritual Growth Mission Statement

_____

_____

My Spiritual Growth Goals

_____

_____

My Spiritual Growth Objectives

_____

_____

_____

Intellectual

Assessing and Developing Your Mission, Goals, and Objectives for Your Intellectual Growth Spoke

Intellectual growth is related to the enhancement of your strategic thinking skills, analysis skills, study skills, and higher-level questioning skills. It is reading, studying, and learning more effectively. It is developing the skills of planning, problem identification, and problem solving. It is enhancing your ability to participate in thoughtful discussions.

Some claim the average person uses less than 10 percent of his or her brain capacity. So we all have room to grow as a thinking person!

The following questions will help you think through what you want to include in the mission, goals, and objectives for the *Intellectual Growth Spoke*. Make a copy of the questions and keep it available in your journal as you focus on developing your mission, goals, and objectives for this dimension of your life.

1. What will intellectual fulfillment look like from my perspective? Is it compatible with God's perspective?

2. What intellectual objectives and activities will help me mature in Christ?

3. What can I do to develop and broaden my intellectual activities?

4. What steps do I need to take to accomplish the objectives I've identified?

5. How will I know my intellectual growth objectives and activities are contributing to a more balanced life for me according to God's standards?

6. How will I know that my intellectual growth objectives and activities are adding to my emotional, physical, and time reserves?

My Intellectual Growth Mission Statement

_____

_____

My Intellectual Growth Goals

_____

_____

My Intellectual Growth Objectives

_____

_____

SOCIAL

Assessing and Developing Your Mission, Goals, and Objectives for Your Social Growth Spoke

Social activities are the "fun" stuff and part of the spice of life. They keep the child in us alive and well. Growing in our ability to be sociable, enjoying other people, and doing social things with family and friends are important steps toward enhancing well-rounded relationships.

The following questions will help you think through what you want to include in the mission, goals, and objectives for the *Social Growth Spoke*. Make a copy of the questions and keep it available in your journal as you focus on developing your mission, goals, and objectives for this dimension of your life.

1. What will social fulfillment look like from my perspective? Is it compatible with God's perspective?

2. What types of social objectives and activities will help me mature in Christ?

3. What can I do to develop and broaden my worthwhile social activities?

4. What steps do I need to take to accomplish the social objectives I've identified?

5. How will I know my social objectives and activities are contributing to a more balanced, bountiful, and beneficial life, according to God's standards?

6. How will I know that my social objectives and activities enhance my emotional, physical, and time reserves?

My Social Growth Mission Statement

_____

_____

My Social Growth Goals

_____

_____

_____

My Social Growth Objectives

_____

_____

RECREATIONAL

Assessing and Developing Your Mission, Goals, and Objectives for Your Recreational Spoke

Recreational activities "restore" our batteries. They provide the platform for us to re-create our sense of grounding and to restore our vitality. They can be solitary, like fishing, jogging, or reading a good book under a shady tree. They can also be very active and involve others, like in a volleyball game.

The following questions will help you think through what you want to include in the mission, goals, and objectives for the *Recreational Spoke.* Make a copy of the questions and keep it available in your journal as you focus on developing your mission, goals, and objectives for this dimension of your life.

1. What will recreational fulfillment look like from my perspective? Is it compatible with God's perspective?

2. What types of recreational objectives and activities will help me mature in Christ?

3. What can I do to develop and broaden my recreational activities?

4. What steps do I need to take to accomplish the objectives I've identified?

5. How will I know my recreational objectives and activities are contributing to a more balanced and bountiful life for me according to God's standards?

6. How will I know that my recreational objectives and activities are increasing my emotional, physical, and time reserves?

My Recreational Growth Mission Statement

_____

_____

My Recreational Growth Goals

_____

_____

_____

My Recreational Growth Objectives

_____

_____

FAMILY

Assessing and Developing Your Mission, Goals, and Objectives for Your *Family Spoke*

Spending time to enhance loving family relationships is an investment. Single or married, family is family. Nurturing and growing these relationships takes an investment of time and talent. It just doesn't happen on its own.

Time together praying, playing, talking, and sharing life's events are all part of being a family. Communicating openly and without rancor builds family relationships. Sharing in the work of the home builds family relationships.

The following questions will help you think through what you want to include in the mission, goals, and objectives for the *Family Spoke.* Make a copy of the questions and keep it available in your journal as you focus on developing your mission, goals, and objectives for this dimension of your life.

1. What will family and/or marriage fulfillment look like from my perspective? Is it compatible with God's perspective?

2. What types of family objectives and activities will help me grow in Christ and better serve the members of my family?

3. What can I do to develop and broaden my worthwhile family activities?

4. What steps do I need to take to accomplish my objectives in this area?

5. How will I know my objectives and activities are contributing to a more balanced and beneficial life for me, according to God's standards?

6. How will I know that my family objectives and activities will honor and glorify God and enhance my emotional, physical, and time reserves?

My Family Growth Mission Statement

_____

_____

My Family Growth Goals

_____

_____

_____

My Family Growth Objectives

_____

_____

_____

CAREER

Assessing and Developing Your Mission, Goals, and Objectives for Your Career Enhancement Spoke

Career and vocation take up a large portion of the employed person's life. Some times too much at the expense of the other dimensions of life! Continuously enhancing and fine-tuning your skills and abilities so you can diligently do timely and "value added" work for the organization that employs you is important. Things like independent study, seminars, workshops, peer-coaching sessions, and video training programs can all help you strengthen your ability to deliver the goods. So can good mentors and a variety of quality work experiences. The more "value added" things you can do excellently, the more valuable you are to an employer.

The following questions will help you think through what you want to include in the mission, goals, and objectives for the *Career Enhancement Spoke*. Make a copy of the questions and keep it available in your journal as you focus on developing your mission, goals, and objectives for this dimension of your life.

1. What will career and work fulfillment look like from my perspective? Is it compatible with God's perspective?

2. What types of career objectives will help me better serve Christ?

3. What can I do to develop and broaden my worthwhile career activities?

4. What steps do I need to take to accomplish the career objectives I've identified?

5. How will I know my career objectives and activities are contributing to a more balanced and beneficial life for me, according to God's standards?

6. How will I know that my career objectives and activities will help me gain and maintain healthy emotional, physical, time, and financial reserves?

My Career Growth Mission Statement

_____

_____

My Career Growth Goals

_____

_____

My Career Growth Objectives

_____

_____

EMOTIONAL GROWTH

Assessing and Developing Your Mission, Goals, and Objectives for Your Emotional Growth Spoke

Emotional growth is related to our movement toward true maturity as a person. A lifelong effort, it is freeing ourselves from the ego-driven, volatile emotions that bind us to thinking irrational thoughts, uttering irrational words, and taking irrational actions. As infants we are physically and emotionally dependent. Unfortunately, we can get stuck there! As we grow and age, we hopefully have opportunities and mentors supporting us in maturing our emotions as we develop an understanding of life's deeper meaning. Given caring feedback and coaching, we will mature emotionally in relationship to authority, personal initiative, and competence, our identity as God's beloved children, our responsiveness to others, and our desire to teach and give to others.

As we grow in emotional maturity, we find ourselves working to understand our negative emotions of fear, anger, hurt, blame, and frustration. We accept them as our own creation and responsibility. We don't blame others or events for the emotions that bind us and blind us. Through God's grace, we learn to love, unconditionally, ourselves and others.

The following questions will help you think through what you want to include in the mission, goals, and objectives for the *Emotional Growth Spoke*. Make a copy of the questions and keep it available in your journal as you focus on developing your mission, goals, and objectives for this dimension of your life.

1. What will emotional maturity look like from my perspective? Is it compatible with God's perspective of being a mature person in Christ?

2. What types of objectives and activities will help me mature in Christ?

3. What can I do to develop and broaden my emotional growth activities?

4. What steps do I need to take to accomplish my growth objectives?

5. How will I know my growth objectives and activities are contributing to a more balanced and beneficial life for me, according to God's standards?

6. How will I know that my emotional growth objectives and activities are adding to my emotional, physical, and time reserves?

My Emotional Growth Mission Statement

_____

_____

My Emotional Growth Goals

_____

_____

My Emotional Growth Objectives

_____

_____

FINANCIAL

Assessing and Developing Your Mission, Goals, and Objectives for Your Financial Spoke

Growth and balance in the financial dimension of your life is best addressed by keeping your eye on *contentment* and *stewardship according to God's standards*. Establishing and maintaining a budget, establishing a regular savings and investment program, living within your means, and giving the "first fruits" of your time, talent, and treasure to God are all elements of your financial spoke. Two excellent resources I'm familiar with that will help you bring balance to this area of your life are: Crown Ministries' *Small Group Financial Study* and *Using Your Money Wisely— Guidelines from Scripture*, by Larry Burkett. Crown Ministries, Inc., can be reached at (407) 331-6000 to get information about the study.

The following questions will help you think through what you want to include in the mission, goals, and objectives for the *Financial Spoke*. Make a copy of the questions and keep it available in your journal as you focus on developing your mission, goals, and objectives for this dimension of your life.

1. What will financial fulfillment look like from my perspective? Is it compatible with God's perspective on contentment?

2. What types of financial objectives and activities will help me better serve Christ?

3. What can I do to develop and broaden my worthwhile financial activities?

4. What steps do I need to take to accomplish my financial goals and objectives?

5. How will I know my financial objectives and activities are contributing to a more balanced life, according to God's standards?

6. How will I know that my financial objectives and activities are the highest and best use of the emotional, physical, and time reserves God has given to me?

My Financial Mission Statement

_____

_____

My Financial Goals

_____

_____

_____

My Financial Objectives

_____

_____

PHYSICAL FITNESS

Assessing and Developing Your Mission, Goals, and Objectives for Your Physical Fitness Spoke

The apostle Paul told us in 2 Corinthians 7:1, "Since we have these promises, dear friends, let us purify ourselves from everything that contaminates body and spirit, perfecting holiness out of reverence for God."

Keeping our physical bodies rested, properly nourished, clean from contamination, and fit to labor for His cause is a personal responsibility. Failing to do so is a sin.

Illicit and promiscuous sexual practices, poor eating, dietary and weight control habits, poor exercise and rest habits, and poor hygiene habits all deter optimum physical fitness and prevent the achievement of a balanced and beneficial life.

The following questions will help you think through what you want to include in the mission, goals, and objectives for the *Physical Fitness Spoke*. Make a copy of the questions and keep it available in your journal as you focus on developing your mission, goals, and objectives for this dimension of your life.

1. What will good physical fitness look like from my perspective? How is it compatible or incompatible with God's perspective?

2. What types of physical fitness objectives and activities will help serve Christ better?

3. What will I do to develop and broaden my worthwhile fitness activities?

4. What steps do I need to take to accomplish the fitness objectives I've identified?

5. How will I know my physical fitness objectives and activities are contributing to a more balanced, bountiful, and beneficial life for me, according to God's standards?

6. How will I know that my fitness objectives and activities are contributing to maintaining healthy personal reserves emotionally, physically, time wise and financially?

My Fitness Mission Statement

_____

_____

My Fitness Goals

_____

_____

_____

My Fitness Objectives

_____

_____

COMMUNITY SERVICE

Assessing and Developing Your Mission, Goals, and Objectives for Your Community Service Spoke

Community. The word has always brought to mind a sense of "coming to unity." The idea that working collaboratively and cooperatively with others for the common good of the community I live in will add to the quality of community life.

Good stewardship is more than dealing with money. It is using our talents and interests for the benefit of others and ourselves. Community service can be serving on a local planning team, getting involved in a service club, discussing problems with elected representatives, coaching a little league team, organizing a cleanup campaign, or a host of other things. If it is truly community service, it is the unconditional giving of your time and talent without expecting anything in return.

The following questions will help you think through what you want to include in the mission, goals, and objectives for the *Community Service Spoke.* Make a copy of the questions and keep it available in your journal as you focus on developing your mission, goals, and objectives for this dimension of your life.

1. What will my community service activities look like from my perspective? Are they compatible with God's perspective on serving others?

2. What types of community involvement will help me mature in Christ?

3. What can I do to develop and broaden my community involvement?

4. What steps do I need to take to accomplish my community service objectives?

5. How will I know my community objectives and supporting activities are contributing to a more balanced, bountiful, and beneficial life for me, according to God's standards?

6. How will I know that my objectives and activities in this area are the highest and best use of my emotional, physical, time, and financial reserves?

My Community Service Statement

_____

_____

My Community Service Goals

_____

_____

_____

My Community Service Objectives

_____

_____

INTEGRITY MANAGEMENT WORKSHOPS
AVAILABLE TO CHRISTIAN ORGANIZATIONS

The how-to, hands-on workshop topics listed below are designed from a biblical perspective to enhance Christian living. Components of the different workshops listed below can be combined and custom tailored to meet the specific needs of groups of Christians who want to extend and master any of the strategies and sets of skills addressed in Millard MacAdam's book, *Intentional Integrity: Aligning Your Life with God's Values.*

PERSONAL FOCUS WORKSHOPS

- Building a Balanced, Bountiful, and Beneficial Life
- Managing a Meaningful Marriage
- Determining Your Values—Establishing Your Boundaries
- Establishing Your Vision and Mission—Achieving Your Goals
- Facilitating a Family PACT: Personal Accountability and Commitment Team
- Following and Leading Others
- Maximizing Your Adaptability
- Resolving and Preventing Conflict
- Communicating Openly, Directly, and Congruently

ORGANIZATION FOCUS WORKSHOPS

- Right Sizing Ethically and Economically
- Mentoring and Coaching Others
- Building High Integrity Teams
- Facilitating Change without Chaos
- Selecting and Deploying the Right People for Maximum Performance
- Facilitating Mutual Accountability

SECULAR VERSION INTEGRITY MANAGEMENT WORKSHOPS

The how-to, hands-on workshop topics listed above are also available to secular business, education, and governmental organizations. They are designed around sound biblical principles to enhance people's character, competence, and commitment to think, say, and do the right things. Each develops practical skills and promotes ethical standards for conduct that will make and save money for all types of small and large organizations and companies.

However, these workshops are designed with a sensitivity to the religiously diverse management and workforce in America and do not contain specific Bible teaching segments. Components of the different workshops listed above can be combined and custom tailored to meet the specific needs of management and work groups that want to extend and master any of the strategies and sets of skills addressed in Dr. MacAdam's book.

For further information, scheduling, or to receive a copy of a descriptive flyer describing the content, benefits, intents and outcomes for any of these workshops please contact:

Dr. Millard MacAdam
Proactive Leadership Consulting & Training
2114 Vista Laredo, Newport Beach, CA 92660-4041
Ph. 714 644-5552, Email: mnmacadam@ad.com, Fax 714 644-6180

ENDNOTES

1. "U.S. Facing Moral Crisis of First Dimension," *World*, May 12, 1986, 6.

2. Nick Poulos, "Have Ethics Worsened in Recent Years?" *Atlanta Journal-Constitution*, November 30, 1986, 1B.

3. Charles Stanley, "Blessed Is the Nation," Audiotape, Atlanta: First Baptist Church, 1994.

4. Warren W. Wiersbe, *The Integrity Crisis* (Nashville, Tenn.: Thomas Nelson, 1991).

5. Tom Haggai, *How The Best Was Won* (Nashville, Tenn.: Thomas Nelson, 1987), 80–83.

6. James E. Burke, Ad Council Speech, November 16, 1983.

7. *Establishing Your Purpose*, Ministry in the Marketplace Series (Knoxville, Tenn.: Vision Foundation Inc.).

8. An article by Robert E. Kelley, "In Praise of Followers," *Harvard Business Review*, November–December 1988, as well as topics Bob Shank has discussed at his Marketplace Commentary meetings in Orange County, have helped me refine these ten hallmarks.

9. Adapted from Millard N. MacAdam's *Beyond Business as Usual: Strategies for Enhancing Ethics and Enterprise*, workshop workbook, © 1991.

10. I want to thank John J. Scherer and Richard N. Bolles in particular for the inspiration their ideas in this area have had on helping me enhance my own adaptability.

I was exposed to Richard Bolles' ideas through his classic book, *What Color Is Your Parachute?* I had the privilege of getting to know John Scherer in a seminar I attended where he gave a paper on the subject entitled, "Job-Related Adaptive Skills: Toward Personal Growth." It was published in the 1980 *Annual Handbook for Group Facilitators*, University Associates.

11. Richard W. Wetherill discovered a simple strategy for surfacing and releasing these wrong thoughts outlined in this chapter. The process has worked for me and lots of others. Mr. Wetherill is the author of several books dealing with The Right-Action Ethic.™ I've outlined elements of his powerful release technique for you in this chapter and used some of the key concepts from his writings as I developed this chapter.

Over the last decade, the concepts and theories of management consultant Peter Block, *Flawless Consulting*, (Learning Concepts, 1981), have helped me understand and deal with resistance in myself and others in more proactive rather than reactive ways. His notions about resistance being a result of perceived loss of control and vulnerability are discussed in this chapter.

The concepts, theories, and work of psychologist Albert Ellis have also helped me better understand my own negative emotions and irrational thinking. Ellis developed the school of psychotherapy that he called Rational-Emotive Therapy. His writing helped me understand the importance of recognizing and correcting my negative internal dialogue in order to experience a balanced life.

12. William J. Bennett, *The Book of Virtues* (Morristown, N.J.: Silver Burdett Press, 1995).

13. Gerald Corey, *Theory and Practice of Counseling and Psychology*, 4th ed. (Pacific Grove, Calif.: Brooks/Cole, 1991), chapter 11. This gives an overview of Albert Ellis's Rational Emotive Therapy and some of the concepts and theories that have helped me develop parts of this chapter.

Richard W. Wetherill, *How to Solve Problems and Prevent Trouble* (Royersford, Penn.: The Alpha Publishing House, 1991). Wetherill's concepts and theories have helped me develop parts of this chapter. The chapter also contains information from the workshop and seminar manual, *Resolving and Preventing Problems*. I helped developed this workshop and seminar for Alpha Publishing House in collaboration with Marie Bothe, founding president of Wetherill and Associates, a manufacturing and sales organization in Royersford, Pennsylvania.

Note: The concept I refer to in this chapter as *CDS, compulsive demand sentences,* is referred to by Richard W. Wetherill in his work as *command phrases* and by Albert Ellis in his work as *negative internal dialogue*. Both Wetherill and Ellis address the importance of events that trigger a connection between a person's negative emotions and the subsequent irrational thinking that gets stored in the subconscious. Both focus on the importance of rational thinking and the importance of a person's "intent" to think straight and do what's right. This intent is critical if a person wishes to remove the irrational thoughts he or she has stored in his or her subconscious mind that trigger inappropriate and dysfunctional behavior.